Pupil Book 6B

Series Editor: Peter Clarke

Authors: Elizabeth Jurgensen, Jeanette Mumford, Sandra Roberts, Linda Glithro

Contents

Unit 5 — Page number

Week 1: Number – Addition, subtraction, multiplication and division, incl. Number and place value

Lesson 1:	Negative numbers	4
Lesson 2:	Negative problems	6
Lesson 3:	Order of operations (1)	8
Lesson 4:	Addition and subtraction review	10

Week 2: Algebra

Lesson 1:	Simple formulae	12
Lesson 2:	Formulae and number sequences	14
Lesson 3:	Building formulae	16
Lesson 4:	Solving problems with unknowns and variables	18

Week 3: Geometry – Properties of shapes

Lesson 1:	Drawing 2-D shapes	20
Lesson 2:	Reasoning about shapes and angles	22
Lesson 3:	Vertically opposite angles	24
Lesson 4:	All about angles	26

Unit 6

Week 1: Number - Multiplication and division

Lesson 1:	Multiplication HTO × TO using partitioning	28
Lesson 2:	Multiplication HTO × TO using the grid method	30
Lesson 3:	Multiplication HTO × TO using the expanded written method	32
Lesson 4:	Multiplication HTO × TO using the formal written method	34

Week 2: Number – Multiplication and division, incl. Decimals

Lesson 1:	Multiplying decimals using mental methods	36
Lesson 2:	Multiplying decimals by a 1-digit number using the grid method	38
Lesson 3:	Multiplying decimals by a 1-digit number using the expanded written method	40
Lesson 4:	Multiplying decimals by a 1-digit number using the formal written method	42

Week 3: Measurement (mass)

Lesson 1:	Mass in action	44
Lesson 2:	Massive masses	46
Lesson 3:	Backpack masses	48
Lesson 4:	Newspaper problems	50

Unit 7

Page number

Week 1: Number – Fractions
- Lesson 1: Adding and subtracting fractions (1) — 52
- Lesson 2: Dividing fractions — 54
- Lesson 3: Multiplying fractions — 56
- Lesson 4: Fraction problems — 58

Week 2: Ratio and proportion
- Lesson 1: Proportion problems — 60
- Lesson 2: Ratio and scale factors — 62
- Lesson 3: Ratio problems — 64
- Lesson 4: Ratio and proportion problems — 66

Week 3: Statistics
- Lesson 1: Water sports centre pie charts — 68
- Lesson 2: Using line graphs — 70
- Lesson 3: Making a survey — 72
- Lesson 4: Finding the mean — 74

Unit 8

Week 1: Number - Multiplication and division
- Lesson 1: Division HTO ÷ TO using the expanded written method — 76
- Lesson 2: Division ThHTO ÷ TO using the expanded written method — 78
- Lesson 3: Division HTO ÷ TO using the formal written method — 80
- Lesson 4: Division ThHTO ÷ TO using the formal written method — 82

Week 2: Number – Multiplication and division, incl. Decimals
- Lesson 1: Dividing decimals using mental methods and the formal written method — 84
- Lesson 2: Dividing decimals using the expanded written method of long division — 86
- Lesson 3: Dividing decimals using the formal written method of long division — 88
- Lesson 4: Solving word problems (3) — 90

Week 3: Measurement (perimeter and area)
- Lesson 1: Perimeter and area — 92
- Lesson 2: Surface area — 94
- Lesson 3: Area of triangles — 96
- Lesson 4: Area of parallelograms — 98

Maths facts — 100

Unit 5, Week 1, Lesson 1

Negative numbers

Use negative numbers and calculate intervals across 0

Challenge 1

1. Count back 10 times from these negative numbers. Write the numbers in your book.

   −9, −10, −11, −12, −13, −14 …

   a −5   b −17   c −24
   d −37   e −49   f −60

2. Use the number line to work out the calculations.

   −10 —————————— 0 —————————— 10

   a 7 − 9   b 3 − 8   c 6 − 10   d 1 − 5   e 10 − 13
   f 4 − 12   g 8 − 11   h 5 − 14   i 2 − 7   j 9 − 14

Challenge 2

1. Work out these calculations. Use jottings to support your working out.

   a 13 − 20   b 17 − 28   c 21 − 30   d 25 − 42
   e 28 − 53   f 30 − 50   g 37 − 55   h 41 − 67

2. Work out these calculation chains. Use jottings to support your working out.

   a 5 − 8 − 3 + 2   b 2 − 11 + 4 − 3
   c 0 − 3 + 6 − 8   d 7 − 12 + 8 − 4
   e 3 − 10 + 7 − 5   f 6 − 13 + 4 − 6
   g 4 − 9 + 10 − 7   h 1 − 14 − 18 + 9

4

3 What is the difference between each pair of numbers?

   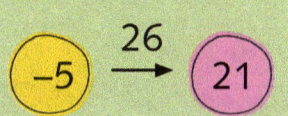

Example

a (−8) (15)   b (−11) (9)   c (−23) (18)   d (−30) (25)

e (−36) (27)   f (−29) (35)   g (−41) (41)   h (−54) (47)

4 Explain how you worked out the difference in Question 3. Why does your method work?

Challenge 3

1 Use a negative number and a positive number to complete each of these calculations.

a ☐ + ☐ = 7   b ☐ + ☐ = 12   c ☐ + ☐ = 15

d ☐ + ☐ = 21   e ☐ + ☐ = 28   f ☐ + ☐ = 36

g ☐ + ☐ = 40   h ☐ + ☐ = 53   i ☐ + ☐ = 24

2 Use two negative numbers to complete each of these calculations.

a ☐ + ☐ = −7   b ☐ + ☐ = −12

c ☐ + ☐ = −15   d ☐ + ☐ = −21

e ☐ + ☐ = −28   f ☐ + ☐ = −36

g ☐ + ☐ = −40   h ☐ + ☐ = −53

3 Use two positive numbers to complete each of these calculations.

a ☐ − ☐ = −7   b ☐ − ☐ = −12

c ☐ − ☐ = −15   d ☐ − ☐ = −21

e ☐ − ☐ = −28   f ☐ − ☐ = −36

g ☐ − ☐ = −40   h ☐ − ☐ = −53

4 Find a partner. Work together to compare your calculations for Questions 1, 2 and 3. Although you probably used different numbers in your calculations, did you still both get the same answers?

Unit 5, Week 1, Lesson 2

Negative problems

Use negative numbers in context and solve multi-step problems

Challenge 1

Read the temperatures on each pair of thermometers. How much has the temperature changed by?

a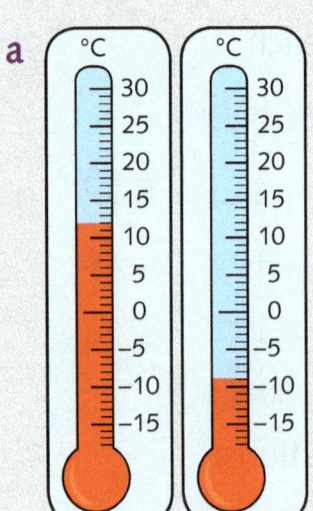

b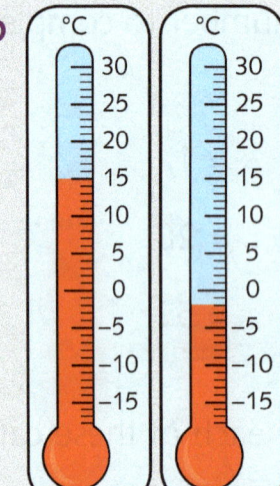

c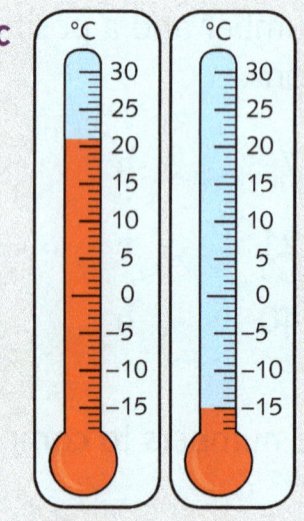

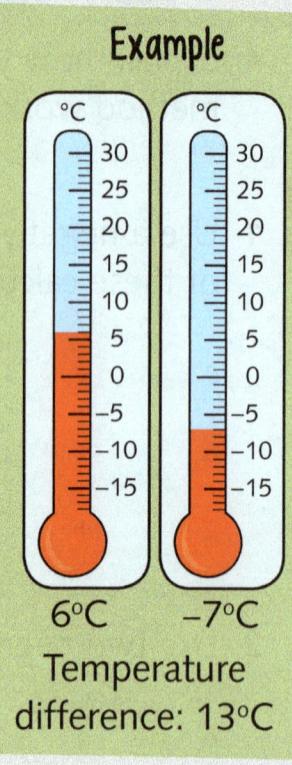

Example

6°C   −7°C

Temperature difference: 13°C

Challenge 2

1 Joe has €40 in his bank account on Monday. Work out how much money Joe has in his account after each event described in questions **a** to **d** below. The answer to each question is the balance that Joe has to start with for the next question.

a On Tuesday, he spends €75 on a new pair of trainers. What is his balance now?

b His mum says he must work to earn the money he owes. So, on Wednesday, he works in a shop and gets paid €27. What is his balance now?

c On Thursday, the next door neighbour asks Joe to mow his lawn and pays him €10. What is his balance now?

d On Friday, his favourite band releases a new album. It costs €8.99 to download. What will his balance be if he buys it?

e Do you think he should download the album now or wait until he earns some more money? Explain your reasons.

6

2 Fahmida has a balance of €45 in her bank account.

a Fahmida's laptop stopped working and she needed another one for school. It cost her €150. What is her balance after buying the laptop?

b She gets a Saturday job to earn some money. Each week she is paid €28. How many weeks will it be until she does not have a negative bank balance?

3 Write a number problem using these amounts. Write the answer to each problem.

a   €18   −€39   +€5   +€12.50   −€11   = €

b   −€30   −€14.30   +€22   +€13   −€2.70   = €

c   €52   −€80   +€45   +€19.50   €27   = €

d   −€14   −€8   −€5.50   −€3.20   €40   = €

Challenge 3

Danny has an overdraft arrangement of €150 with his bank, so his balance can be −€150. Copy Danny's bank statement and fill in the missing balances in the final column.

Date	Payment type and details	Paid out	Paid in	Balance
02 Jan	Balance brought forward			−18.90
05 Jan	Shoe shop	€88.50		
11 Jan	Pizza	€10.00		
16 Jan	Phone bill	€29.97		
30 Jan	Wages		€50.00	
31 Jan	Birthday cheque		€45.00	
31 Jan	Cinema	€12.00		
Balance carried forward				

Unit 5, Week 1, Lesson 3

Order of operations (1)

Use knowledge of the order of operations to carry out calculations involving the four operations

Use the BODMAS rule to work out the answers to these calculations.

a 6 + (13 – 4)
b 5 + (19 – 3)
c 6 + (15 – 5)
d 8 + (14 – 6)
e 7 + (14 – 8)
f 10 – (4 + 2)
g 20 – (9 + 5)
h 20 – (8 – 2)
i 2 × (5 + 4)
j 5 × (7 + 4)
k 5 × (18 – 8)
l 10 × (3 + 6)

Rule

The order of operations is:
B   Brackets
O   Orders (e.g. 4^2)
DM   Division and Multiplication
AS   Addition and Subtraction

The way to remember this is:
BODMAS

1 Use the BODMAS rule to work out the answers to these calculations.

a 6 × 4 + 45
b (9 + 4) × 10
c 92 – (10 × 5)
d 12 ÷ 3 + 18
e 12 × 12 + 9
f 10 × 4 ÷ 2
g 160 – 5 × 6
h 250 – 100 ÷ 2
i 69 – 4 + 9 + 15
j (56 + 56) + 8 ÷ 2
k (32 + 46) × 5 × 2
l (18 – 2) × (4 + 3)

2 Design a poster to help you remember the BODMAS rule. Make it memorable for you!

3 Using the numbers and operations below, with either one or two sets of brackets, how many different answers can you make?

Challenge 3

1 Write out each calculation twice. In each one, put brackets in a different place so each gives a different value.

a 15 − 4 × 2
b 9 × 4 + 6
c 12 ÷ 2 + 4
d 4 + 6 × 7
e 22 + 3 × 4
f 5 × 2 × 3 + 4
g 13 + 24 × 3 − 15
h 25 − 43 − 17 + 9
i 12 × 6 + 5 ÷ 10
j 100 ÷ 4 × 3 − 21

2 Fill in the missing numbers.

a 4 × ☐ − (☐ − ☐) = 80

b 4 × ☐ + 4 × 4 = 80

c 4 × (☐ × ☐) × ☐ = 80

d 4 × ☐ − (4 × ☐) − (☐ × ☐) = 80

3 Fill in the missing numbers.

a 6 × (☐ + ☐) × ☐ + (☐ − ☐) = 200

b 6 × ☐ − (☐ − ☐) = 200

c 6 × ☐ − (6 × ☐) − (☐ × ☐) = 200

d 6 × (☐ ÷ ☐) + (☐ + ☐) = 200

Unit 5, Week 1, Lesson 4

Addition and subtraction review

- Add and subtract mentally and using the formal written methods
- Solve problems involving addition, subtraction, multiplication and division

1. Work out these calculations, deciding the best method to use. Be sure to estimate the answer first and check your answer with your estimate.

   a 45 872 + 6721
   b 31 761 + 5000
   c 67 541 − 42 961
   d 74 293 − 30 000
   e 365 297 − 4000
   f 287 651 + 50 000
   g 751 296 − 42 807
   h 482 396 + 628 385

2. Solve these problems.

   a The Ticket Centre sells two peak time first-class return tickets to Australia for €15 870, and four tickets for €29 500. The Gould family buy two sets of two tickets, while the Herne family buy a ticket for four. How much more does the Gould family pay than the Herne family?

   b At the cinema, 3782 children go to see the new film. Each ticket costs €4. How much money does the cinema take?

   c One week a gardener earns €630 for his work. If he charges €18 an hour, how many hours did he work that week?

1. Work out these calculations, deciding the best method to use. Be sure to estimate the answer first and check your answer with your estimate.

   a 4 873 207 + 372 206
   b 7 286 296 − 5382
   c 3 287 461 + 70 000
   d 5 762 286 − 8100
   e 2 762 067 − 36 842
   f 482 295 + 300 000
   g 2 265 207 + 230 000
   h 726 296 − 18 000

2 Solve these problems.

a Three friends go into a bookshop. Salma buys a cookbook and a novel. She pays €20.75. Isla buys the same novel and a dictionary. Her bill comes to €26.65. Josh buys the cookbook and the dictionary and pays €30.90. What is the price of each book?

b One film made €4 762 359, a second film made double this, and another film made €781 207. What was the total money taken for these three films?

c The school puts on a play to raise money. Tickets cost €12. A total of 98 people buy full-price tickets and 243 people buy half-price tickets. How much money is raised?

Challenge 3

The surveyor is working out the costs to build some new houses. These are her prices.

Four-bedroom houses at €356 400

Three-bedroom houses at €287 695

Two-bedroom houses at €207 830

1 The builder has €5 000 000 to spend.

a If he only builds one kind of house, how many of each one will he be able to build?

b If he builds approximately the same number of each kind of house, how many of each one can he build?

Hint
As the builder needs the money he decides to round the prices to the nearest euro.

2 The builder wants to make a nice profit when he sell his houses. So for the asking price of each house he has decided on the following:

i Four-bedroom houses: building cost + 20%

ii Three-bedroom houses: building cost +10%

iii Two-bedroom houses: building cost +15%

Work out the asking price of each type of house.

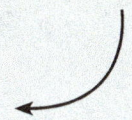

Unit 5, Week 2, Lesson 1

Simple formulae

Use simple formulae

Example
$16 + x = 20$
$x = 20 - 16$
$x = 4$

Challenge 1

1. Solve these missing number equations by finding the value of the letter in each one.

   a $12 + p = 18$ b $15 + y = 24$ c $22 - t = 20$ d $50 - 2m = 20$

2. The formula for the distance D in kilometres travelled by a car in t hours is $D = 50t$. How far does the car travel in:

   a 2 hours?   b 5 hours?   c 8 hours?

3. The formula to convert Dollars to Euros is $1 = 0·7€. How many Euros are in:

   a $20?   b $100?   c $500?

Example
$26 + x = 40$
$x = 40 - 26$
$x = 14$
$3c = 12$
$c = 12 \div 3$
$c = 4$

Challenge 2

1. Solve these missing number equations by finding the value of the letter in each one.

   a $45 + y = 82$ b $34 + m = 71$ c $4n = 408$ d $6p = 450$

2. There are 20 seats in each row at the cinema. How many seats are there in:

   a 2 rows?   b 10 rows?   c n rows?

3. A box contains 24 bottles of water. How many bottles are there in:

   a 3 boxes?   b 5 boxes?   c n boxes?

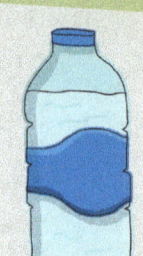

4. There are 6 apples in a pack. If N is the total number of apples, write a formula, beginning '$N =$ ' to show how many apples there are in p packs.

5. Biscuits are packed in boxes of 8. If B is the total number of biscuits, write a formula to show how many biscuits are in t boxes.

12

6 The length of this line is *x* cm: ─────────
   Write a formula for the length *L* of other lines if they are:

   a 4 cm shorter than this line
   b 3 times the length of this line
   c 6 cm longer than this line
   d 2 cm more than double the length of the line

7 Sam does a paper round. Each week she earns €10 plus 25c for each paper delivered. Write a formula in euros for her weekly income. You will need to choose a suitable letter to use for her total weekly earnings and a letter for the number of papers delivered.

8 The formula to calculate average speed is $s = \frac{d}{t}$ where *s* is the average speed, *d* is the distance travelled and *t* is the time taken. Use the formula to calculate the average speed in kilometres per hour for the following cars. Then round the speed to the nearest 10 km/h.

   a Car A travelled 98 kilometres in 2 hours.
   b Car B travelled 164 kilometres in 4 hours.
   c Car C travelled 175 kilometres in 5 hours.

Challenge 3

Example
$3x + 47 = 65$
$3x = 65 - 47$
$3x = 18$
$x = 18 \div 3$
$x = 6$

1 Solve these missing number equations by finding the value of the letter in each one.

   a $3p + 55 = 82$
   b $3z - 12 = 168$
   c $3r + 14 = 47$
   d $4n + 1 = 1001$
   e $6q - 30 = 42$
   f $12a - 12 = 72$

2 Work with a partner and decide who is A and who is B. Take turns to roll the dice and calculate your score using the formulas below. *d* is the value on the dice you rolled:

   $A = 3 + d$ $B = 2d$

You will need:
• 1–6 dice

After five turns each, add up your scores. The winner is the player with the larger score. Which formula wins most often? Can you work out why this is?

Unit 5, Week 2, Lesson 2

Formulae and number sequences

- Generate and describe linear number sequences
- Use simple formulae

Challenge 1

1 Use the pictures to answer the questions.

   a Draw the next two pictures.

   b Copy and complete the table for up to 10 geostrips.

Geostrips	1	2	3	4	5					
Fasteners	0	1	2							

   c How many fasteners would be needed to join:

      i 10 geostrips?   ii 50 geostrips?   iii 100 geostrips?

   d Write a rule in words for the number of fasteners required for any number of geostrips.

   e If F = number of fasteners and g = number of geostrips, which formula describes the rule correctly? $F = g$ $F = g + 1$ $F = g - 1$

2 6 people can sit around a rectangular table.

   a To seat more people two identical tables are pushed together, joining by the short edge. Draw diagrams to show how many people can sit around 2 tables and 3 tables.

   b Draw a table similar to that in Question 1 to show the number of people that can be seated at 1 to 8 tables.

   c Write a formula for n tables.

Challenge 2

1 Use the pictures to answer the questions.

a Copy and complete the table for up to 10 triangles.

Triangles	1	2	3	4	5					
Geostrips	3	5	7							
Fasteners	3	4	5							

b How many geostrips would be needed for:

    i 15 triangles?   ii 40 triangles?   iii 95 triangles?

c Write a rule in words and a formula for working out the number of geostrips (*N*) needed for any number of triangles (*t*).

d What is the formula for the number of fasteners (*F*) required for any number of triangles (*t*)?

2 For each sequence below, calculate the next three terms and then work out the formula for the *n*th term.

Example

Term	1	2	3	4	5	6	7	*n*th
Number	3	5	7	9	11	13	15	$2n+1$

a

Term	1	2	3	4	5	6	7	*n*th
Number	13	23	33	43				

b

Term	1	2	3	4	5	6	7	*n*th
Number	1	4	7	10				

Challenge 3

Mathematicians use this formula to calculate the number of diagonals for a polygon:

You will need:
- 1 cm squared paper
- ruler

number of diagonals, $D = \dfrac{n(n-3)}{2}$ where *n* = number of sides

a Draw a square, a regular pentagon and a regular hexagon and draw in all the diagonals. Check that the formula gives the correct answer for a square, a pentagon and a hexagon by substituting the value of *n* for each one.

b Use the formula to calculate how many diagonals a regular octagon has. Then draw an octagon with all diagonals to check that it is correct.

c A hectagon is a regular polygon with 100 sides. How many diagonals does it have?

Unit 5, Week 2, Lesson 3

Building formulae

- Express missing number problems algebraically
- Use simple formulae

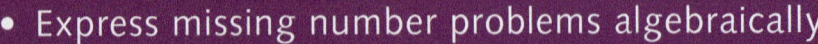

Challenge 1

1. The cost of hiring a motorboat is €60 plus €40 per hour.

    a Write a formula to show the total cost of hiring the motorboat.

    b Calculate the total cost of hiring the motorboat for 3 hours.

    c You have €260. For how long can you hire the motorboat?

2. Write each secret number puzzle as an equation and then solve it.

    a When I add 12 to my secret number the answer is 16.

    b When I double my secret number and add 1, the answer is 13.

    c When I multiply my secret number by 4 and take away 7, the answer is 9.

Challenge 2

1. In a television quiz, four teams each begin with €x and answer 10 questions. For each correct answer the team is given €50. For each question that the team gets wrong or cannot answer, they lose €75.

    a Write equations to show how much each team has at the end of the quiz if:

    i Team A answers 8 questions correctly and 2 incorrectly.

    ii Team B answers all 10 questions correctly.

    iii Team C answers 6 questions correctly and 4 incorrectly.

    iv Team D answers half of the questions correctly.

    b How much does each team take home if x = €1000?

2 A car salesperson earns €1000 a month basic pay plus an extra €100 for each car that he sells.

  a Write a formula for his monthly pay. Use *P* for his monthly pay and *n* for the number of cars he sells.

  b How much does he earn in a month if he sells:

    i 12 cars?   ii 7 cars?

  c How many cars has he sold if his monthly pay is:

    i €2900?   ii €1300?

1 Remember that the angles in a triangle add up to 180°.

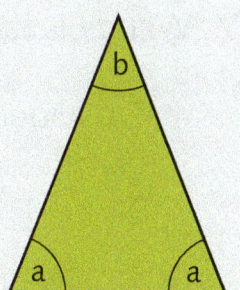

  a Write the formula that shows the sum of the angles in the triangle shown is equal to 180°.

  b If one angle in the triangle shown is 30°, what could the other angles be? Sketch and label the two possible triangles.

  c Choose a different acute angle and sketch and label the two possible triangles.

2 Work with a partner. Imagine you work in the travel industry. Travel agents might use formulae:

  • to work out the total cost of flights for a family

  • to change money in euros into other currencies

  • to work out the total cost of a hotel stay (think about the number of rooms and the number of nights).

Work out some formulae to help with these calculations. You may be able to think of more formulae that travel agents might use.

Unit 5, Week 2, Lesson 4

Solving problems with unknowns and variables

- Find pairs of numbers that satisfy an equation with two unknowns
- List possible combinations of two variables

Challenge 1

1 On a distant planet there are some strange creatures. Triplers have 3 heads and doublers have 2 heads. An astronaut can see 21 heads in total.

  a Write an equation for the number of heads.
  b Work out how many doublers and triplers there could be.

2 Wendy is taking parcels to the post office.

  a On Monday, Wendy takes 2 parcels to the post office. Parcel A weighs 8 kg less than Parcel B. Their total mass is 34 kg. Find the mass of each parcel.

  b On Wednesday, Wendy has 3 parcels to post. 2 weigh the same and the other is 5 kg heavier. Their total mass is 26 kg. Find a possible mass for each parcel.

  c On Friday, Wendy takes 5 parcels to the post office. 3 parcels have the same mass. The other 2 are twice as heavy as the first 3 when weighed together. The total mass is 45 kg. Find the mass of each parcel.

Challenge 2

1 You have a pile of 5c and 10c coins. How many different ways can you make 50c, using combinations of 5c and 10c coins? Use the formula below to help you.

$10a + 5b = 50$ where a = number of 10c coins and b = number of 5c coins.

2 On a distant planet, there are some strange creatures. Tripos have 3 legs and sevenees have 7 legs. An astronaut counts 55 legs in total. How many of each type of creature could there be?

3 Thomas is 2 years older than his sister, Amelia. In 5 years' time, the sum of their ages will be 30 years. Find their ages now.

4 Make up a problem like Question 3 and try it out on a partner.

5 A school enters a national quiz. Here are the rules:
   - There are 8 children in a team.
   - There must be at least 2 boys and at least 2 girls in the team.

   List the combinations of boys and girls that are possible for the school's team.

Challenge 3

1 On a distant planet, there are some strange creatures with long antennae. The purple ones have 3 antennae. The yellow ones have 5 antennae. The blue ones have 11 antennae. A scanner counts exactly 50 antennae. How many of each type of creature could there be?

2 You have €100 in €5 notes and €2 coins. You can make €100 using various combinations of €5 notes and €2 coins.

   a Write a formula to show the various combinations of €5 notes and €2 coins you could have.

   b List all the possible combinations. Try to be systematic in your approach.

Hint
Look at the formula in Challenge 2, Question 1.

Unit 5, Week 3, Lesson 1

Drawing 2-D shapes

Draw 2-D shapes accurately and use conventional markings for lines and angles

You will need:
- ruler
- protractor

 Challenge 1

1. Use your ruler and protractor to construct the rectangle ABCD using the instructions below.

    - Draw line DC 8 cm long.
    - Draw an angle of 90° at C.
    - Draw line CB 4 cm long.
    - Draw an angle of 90° at D.
    - Draw line DA 4 cm long.
    - Join A to B to complete the rectangle.

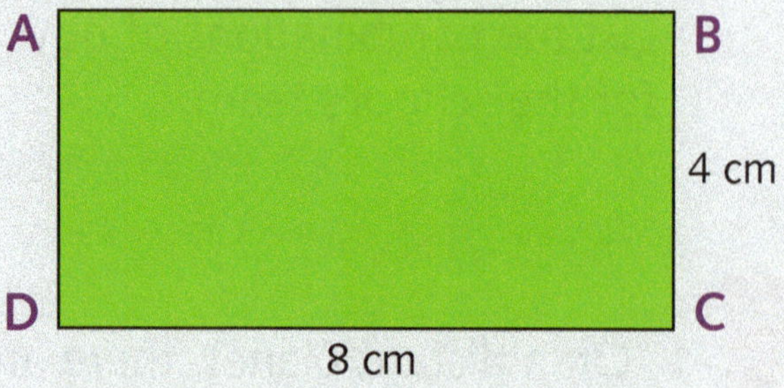

2. Use single and double dashes to mark each pair of equal sides.

3. Use a small square to mark each right angle.

Challenge 2

1. Use your ruler and protractor to construct the triangle ABC using the instructions below.

    - Draw line CB 8 cm long.
    - Draw an angle of 60° at C.
    - Draw line CA 5 cm long.
    - Join A to B to complete the triangle.

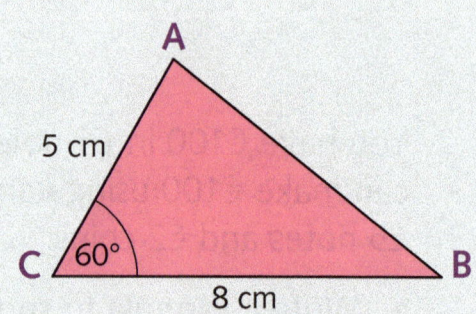

2. Construct the triangle KLM.

    a. Measure and label the size of the angle at K and at L to the nearest degree.

    b. Measure and label the length of the line KL to the nearest millimetre.

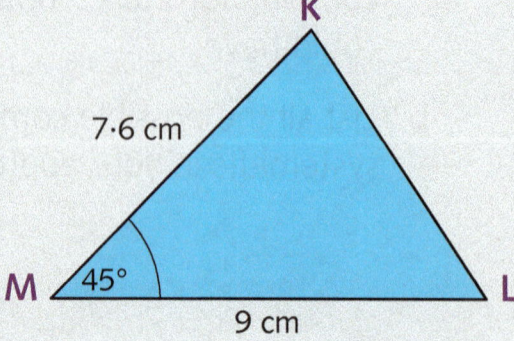

20

3 Construct the right-angled triangle PQR.

   a Measure and label the length of the line PQ to the nearest millimetre.

   b Measure and label the size of the angle at P and at Q to the nearest degree.

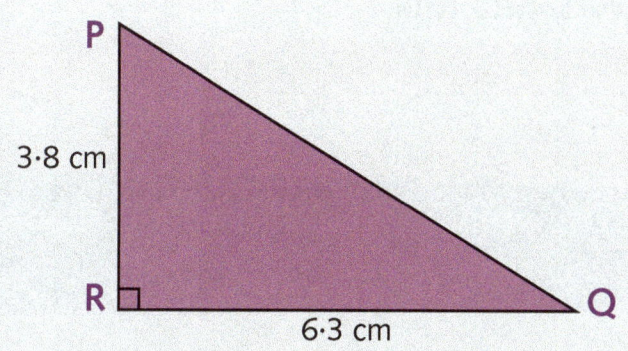

4 Construct the trapezium ABCD using the instructions below.

   • Draw line DC 10·5 cm long.
   • Draw an angle of 90° at D.
   • Draw line DA 6·6 cm long.
   • Draw an angle of 42° at C.
   • Draw an angle of 90° at A.
   • Mark the vertex B at the intersection of the lines drawn from the vertices A and C.

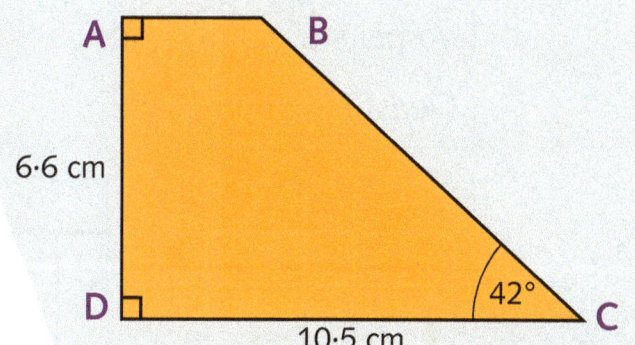

   a Measure and label the lengths of the lines AB and BC to the nearest millimetre.

   b Measure and label the size of the angle at B to the nearest degree.

5 Use the information in the diagram to construct the parallelogram PQRS.

   a Use the symbols > and >> to mark the pairs of parallel lines.

   b Use single and double arcs to mark each pair of equal angles.

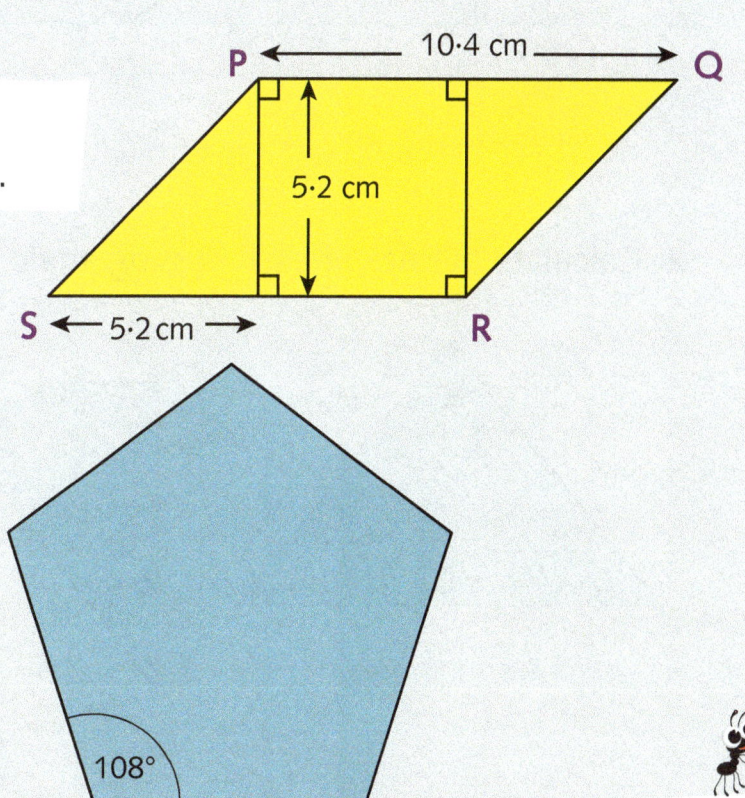

Challenge 3

Use the information in the diagram to construct a regular pentagon.

21

Unit 5, Week 3, Lesson 2

Reasoning about shapes and angles

Use properties to classify 2-D shapes and find the missing angles in 2-D shapes

1 Write the letters of the shapes with these properties:

   a Two pairs of parallel sides   b Opposite angles equal
   c At least one right angle   d One line of symmetry

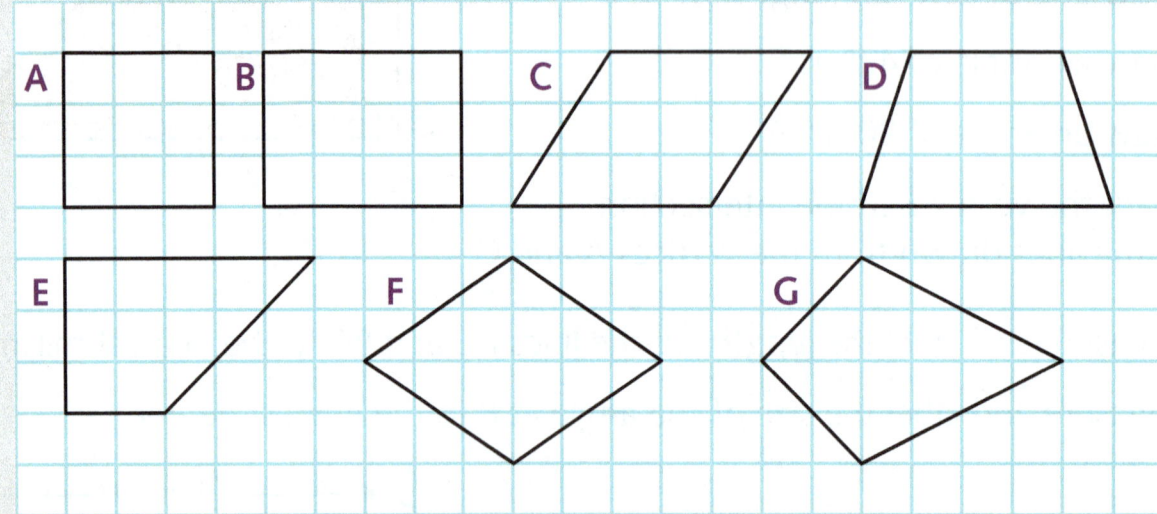

2 Calculate the size of each missing angle.

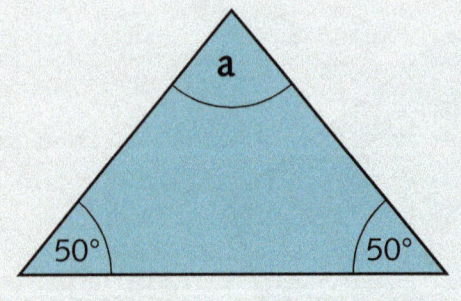

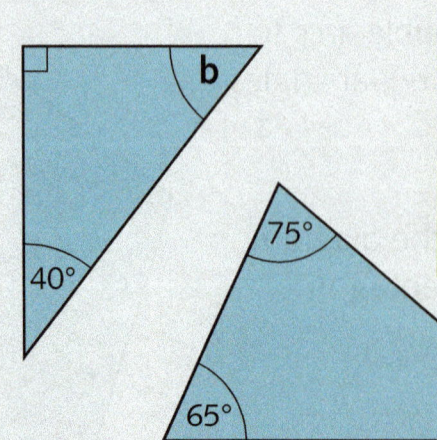

Example

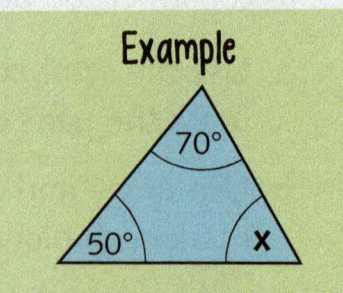

x = 180° − (50° + 70°)
  = 180° − 120°
  = 60°

Challenge 2

1 Look at the shapes A to G in Challenge 1. Write the letters of the shapes with these properties:

   a Diagonals bisect all the angles
   b One pair of parallel sides
   c No axis of symmetry
   d No pairs of perpendicular sides

2 Calculate the size of the angles marked with letters on each triangular sail.

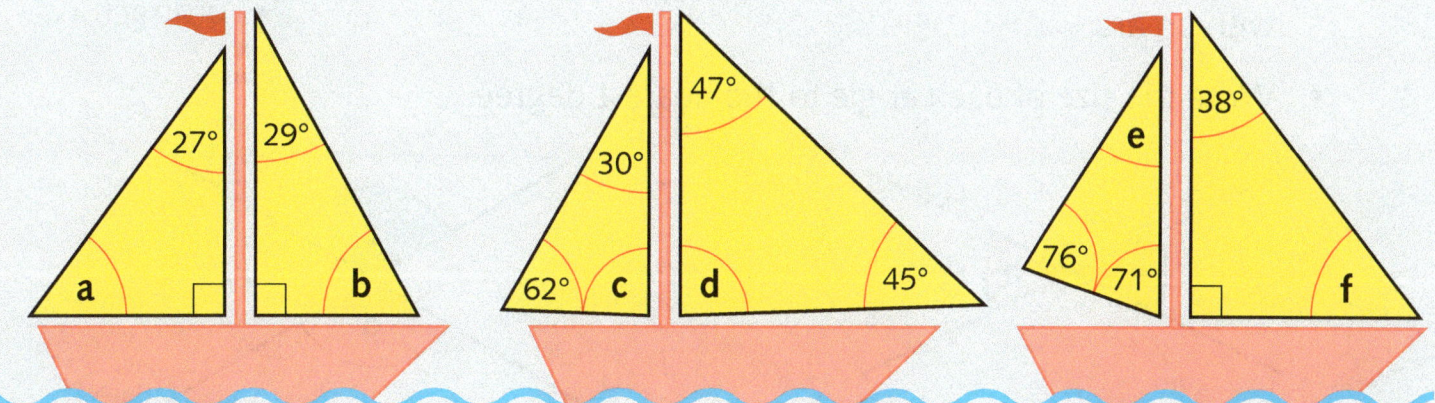

3 Calculate the size of the missing angles in each shape.

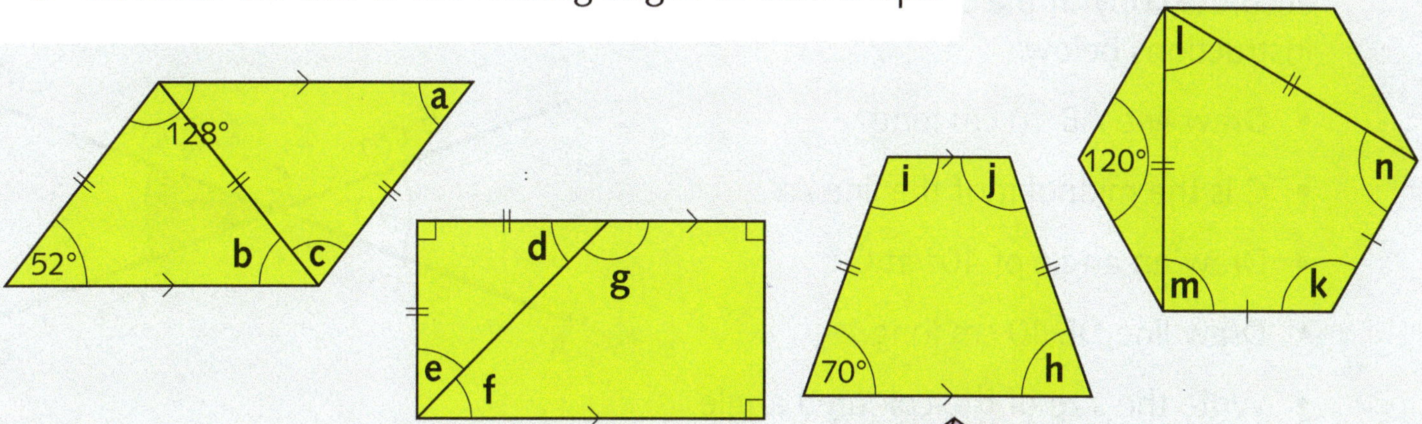

Challenge 3

The angles in a regular pentagon measure 108°. Angle **a** measures 72°. Calculate the size of the marked angles **b** to **l**.

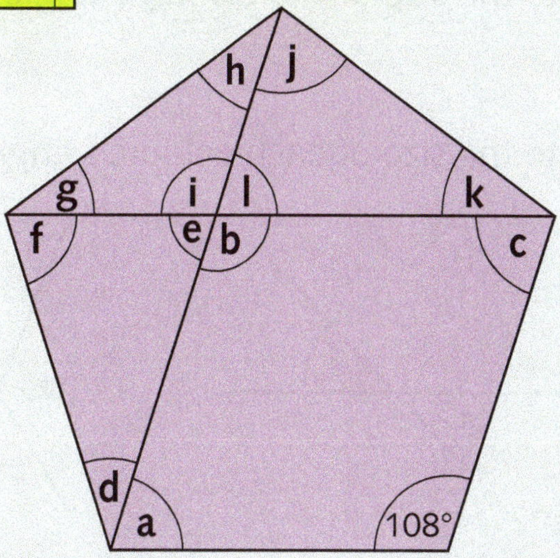

23

Unit 5, Week 3, Lesson 3

Vertically opposite angles

Identify and name vertically opposite angles

Challenge 1

1 For each diagram:
- Use your protractor to measure the two angles marked with an arc.
- Write the size of each angle to the nearest degree.

You will need:
- ruler
- protractor

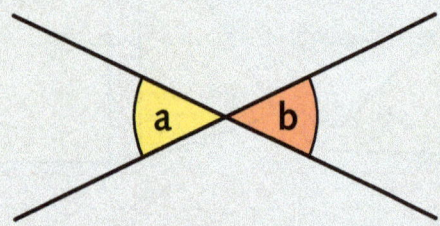

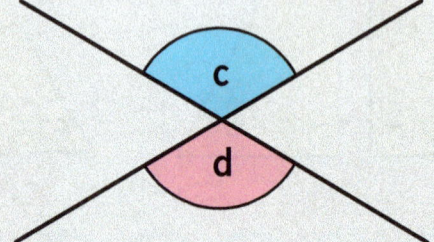

2 Use your ruler and protractor to make an accurate copy of the diagram, using the instructions below.
- Draw line AB 10 cm long.
- C is the midpoint of the line AB.
- Draw an angle of 40° at C.
- Draw line DE 10 cm long.
- Write the size of the coloured angle.

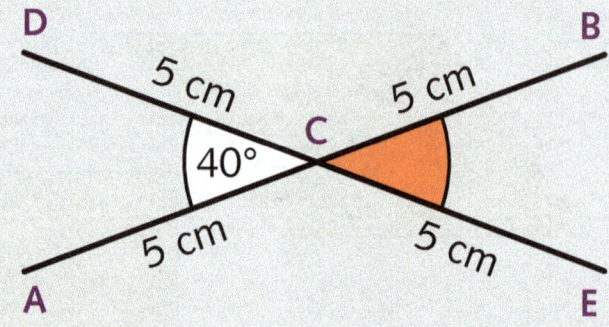

Challenge 2

1 Calculate the size of each coloured angle, **a** to **s**.

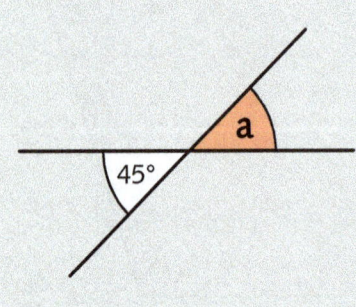

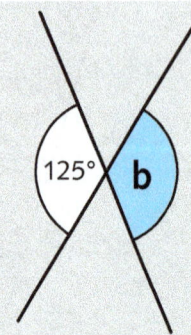

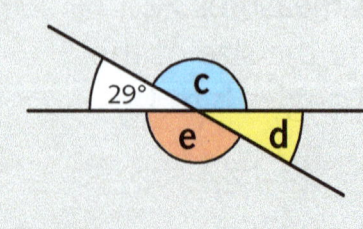

24

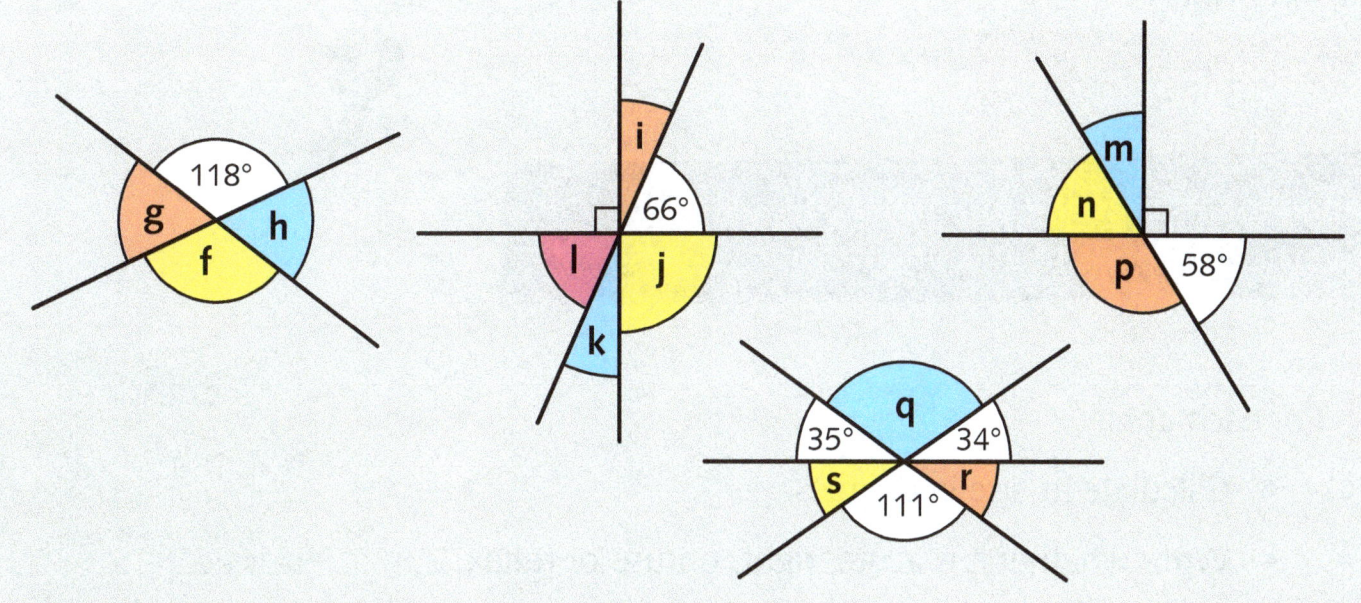

2 The diagram below shows the angles **a**, **b**, **c** and **d** at the intersection of two straight lines.

- Copy the table showing three values for angle **a**.
- For each value of angle **a**, calculate the size of angles **b**, **c** and **d**.

Angle a	Angle b	Angle c	Angle d
65°			
78°			
23°			

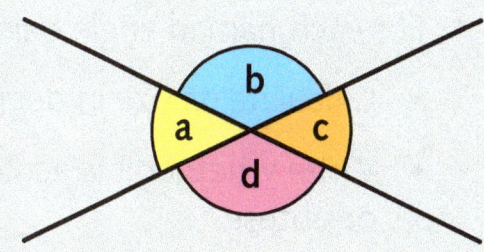

Challenge 3

Use the information in the diagram to calculate the size of each angle, **a** to **f**.

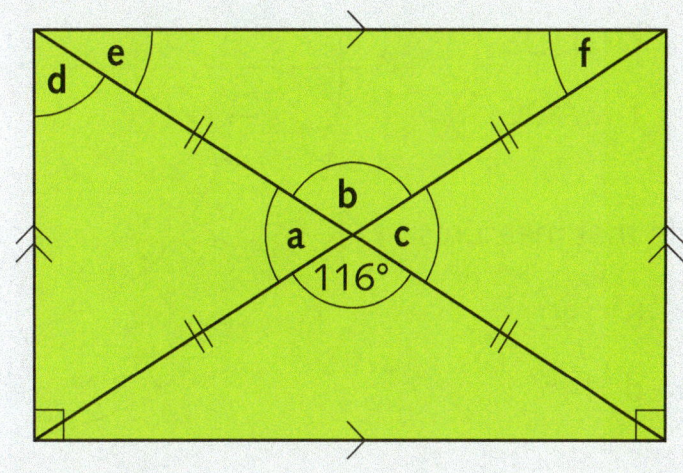

25

Unit 5, Week 3, Lesson 4

All about angles

Name angles meeting at a point, on a straight line or vertically opposite and find missing angles

Challenge 1

For each angle:
- Calculate its size in degrees.
- Write whether it is acute, right, obtuse or reflex.

Example
b = 180° − 140°
= 40°
b is acute

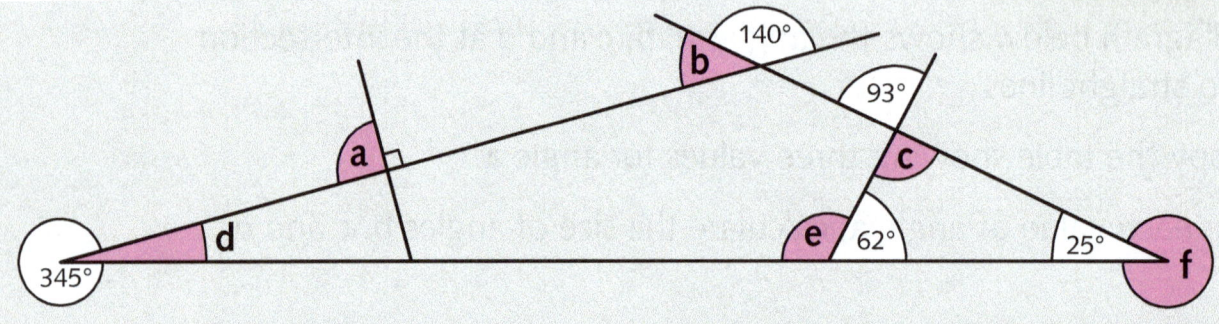

Challenge 2

1 For each named angle below:
- Calculate its size in degrees.
- Write whether it is acute, right or obtuse.

a ∠AOB
b ∠BOC
c ∠COD
d ∠DOE
e ∠FOA
f ∠AOC

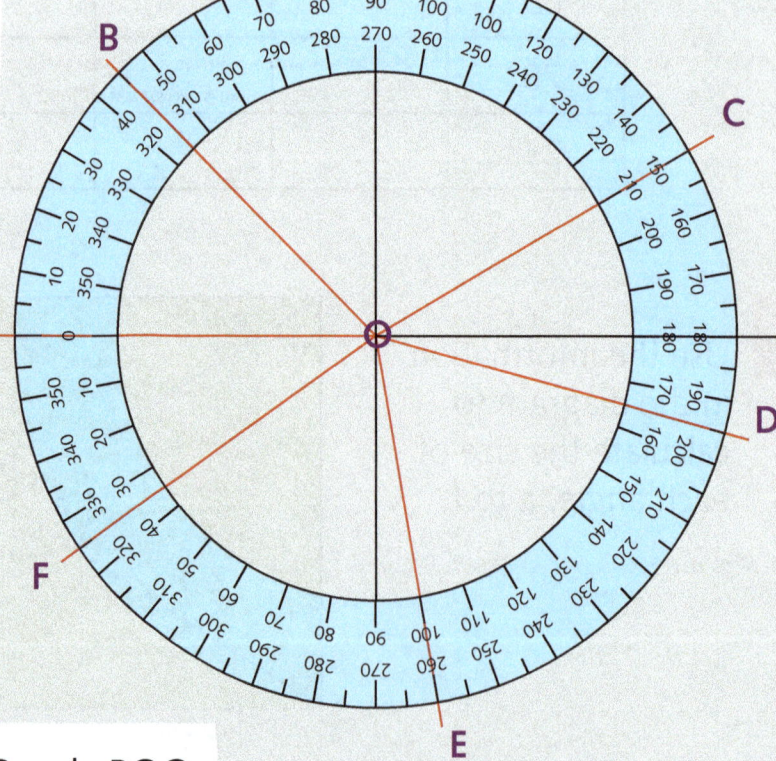

2 Name the angle that measures:

a 100°
b 130°
c 195°
d 145°

3 Find the difference between ∠AOC and ∠BOC.

26

4 PQ is a straight line.

   a Calculate the size of ∠r and ∠s when ∠r = ∠s.
   b Calculate the size of ∠s when ∠r = 38°.

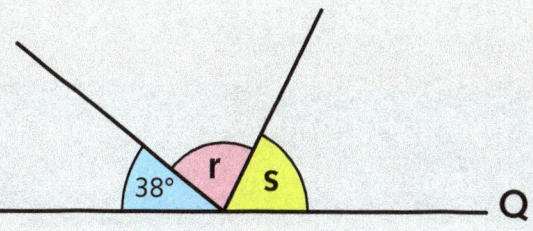

5 Name and calculate the size of each shaded angle that meets at a point.

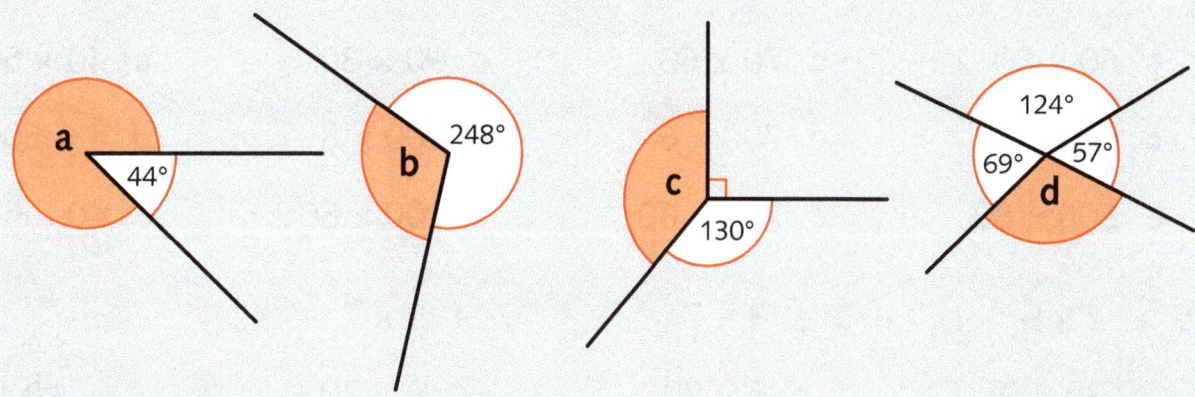

6 Calculate the missing angles **a** to **i** in these diagrams of pairs of intersecting straight lines.

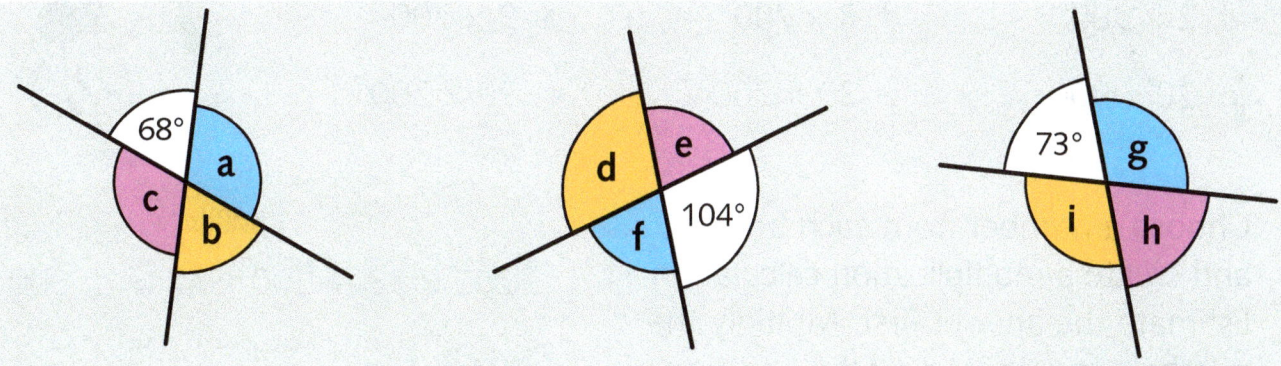

Challenge 3 Measure each acute angle then calculate the reflex angle.

You will need:
- ruler
- protractor

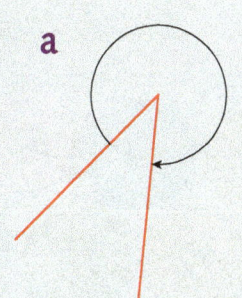
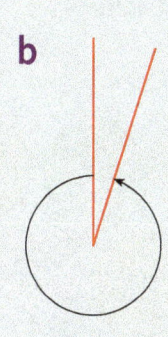
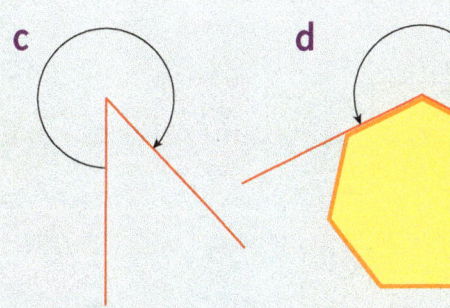

27

Unit 6, Week 1, Lesson 1

Multiplication HTO × TO using partitioning

- Use partitioning to calculate HTO × TO
- Estimate and check the answer to a calculation

Challenge 1

1. a 6 × 8
   b 60 × 8
   c 60 × 80
   d 600 × 8
   e 600 × 80

2. a 7 × 6
   b 70 × 6
   c 70 × 60
   d 700 × 6
   e 700 × 60

3. a 9 × 8
   b 90 × 8
   c 90 × 80
   d 900 × 8
   e 900 × 80

4. a 4 × 5
   b 4 × 50
   c 40 × 50
   d 4 × 500
   e 40 × 500

5. a 2 × 9
   b 20 × 9
   c 20 × 90
   d 2 × 900
   e 20 × 900

6. a 3 × 7
   b 3 × 70
   c 30 × 70
   d 3 × 700
   e 30 × 700

7. a 9 × 7
   b 9 × 70
   c 90 × 70
   d 9 × 700
   e 90 × 700

Challenge 2

1. Choose a number from each box and create a multiplication calculation. Estimate the answer first. Multiply the numbers together using the partitioning method. Then compare your answer with your estimate. Choose different numbers each time. Write at least eight calculations.

Example

263 × 38 → 300 × 40 = 12 000

263 × 38
= (200 × 38) + (60 × 38) + (3 × 38)
= 7600 + 2280 + 114
= 9994

28

2 Use the clues to work out each HTO × TO calculation.

a ☐☐☐ × ☐☐ = 8820

Clue:
The 3-digit number:	The 2-digit number:
• is a multiple of 5	• is a multiple of 6
• is between 200 and 250	• is a square number

b ☐☐☐ × ☐☐ = 8436

Clue:
The 3-digit number:	The 2-digit number:
• is an even number	• is less than 20
• has the same digit in all three place values	• is a prime number

c ☐☐☐ × ☐☐ = 15 504

Clue:
The 3-digit number:	The 2-digit number:
• has consecutive digits in ascending order	• has consecutive digits in ascending order
• is less than 500	• is less than 50

d ☐☐☐ × ☐☐ = 7290

Clue:
• The 3-digit number is an even number less than 200.	• The 2-digit number is less than 50.
• The sum of the three digits in the 3-digit number is 9.	• The sum of the two digits in the 2-digit number is 9.

Challenge 3

Johan tried to work out the answer to 39 × 24 on his calculator but he found that the 9 key on the calculator was broken. He used four different methods to find his answer:

38 × 24 = 912
add 1 × 24 = 24
so 912 + 24 (mentally) = 936

37 × 24 = 888
add 2 × 24 = 48
so 888 + 48 = 936

40 × 24 = 960
subtract 1 × 24 = 24
so 960 − 24 (mentally) = 936

42 × 24 = 1008
subtract 3 × 24 = 72
so 1008 − 72 = 936

Explore methods of finding the answer to these calculations without using the 9 key on the calculator.
Record your methods.

You will need:
• calculator

a 69 × 58

b 49 × 29

c 99 × 38

d 93 × 49

e 96 × 96

f 69 × 99

g 99 × 99

h 59 × 19

29

Unit 6, Week 1, Lesson 2

Multiplication HTO × TO using the grid method

- Use partitioning and the grid method to calculate HTO × TO
- Estimate and check the answer to a calculation

Challenge 1

Write a multiplication number sentence and answer for each number in the snowflakes.

Challenge 2

1 Approximate the answer to each calculation.

Example
264 × 38 → 300 × 40 = 12 000

a 326 × 38
b 452 × 19
c 612 × 26
d 784 × 23
e 357 × 46
f 184 × 15
g 772 × 55
h 394 × 88

30

2 For each of the calculations in Question 1 use the grid method to work out the answer.
   Then compare your answer with your approximation in Question 1.

Example

264 × 38

×	200	60	4
30	6000	1800	120
8	1600	480	32

```
  7920
+ 2112
------
 10032
     1
```

3 As Mrs Keft was marking Natasha's work, she spilt ink over her exercise book. Look carefully at Natasha's work to discover what the two HTO × TO calculations are.

a   4⬛ × 37 = 17 094

×	400	⬛	⬛
30	12 000	⬛	60
7	2800	⬛	14

```
  13 860
+  3 234
--------
  17 094
       1
```
✓

b   26⬛ × 2⬛ = 7532

×	200	60	⬛
20	4000	1200	⬛
⬛	1600	480	⬛

```
  5380
+ 2152
------
  7532
     1
```
✓

Challenge 3

1 Two 2-digit numbers multiply to give an answer of 196. Find the two missing numbers.

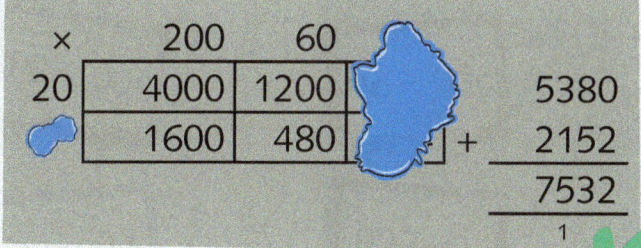

□□ × □□ = 196

2 What is the smallest 2-digit number that can be multiplied by itself to give a 4-digit answer?

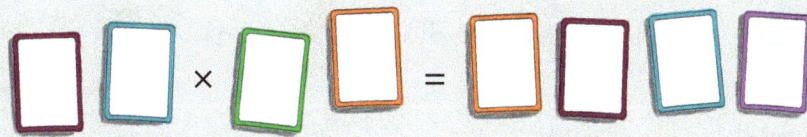

Hint

17 multiplied by itself gives a 3-digit answer.

17 × 17 = 289

31

Unit 6, Week 1, Lesson 3

Multiplication HTO × TO using the expanded written method

- Use the expanded written method to calculate HTO × TO
- Estimate and check the answer to a calculation

Challenge 1

1 Work out the answer to each calculation mentally.

a 6 × 70
b 800 × 40
c 40 × 90
d 500 × 8
e 500 × 50
f 300 × 80
g 700 × 8
h 60 × 80
i 7 × 900
j 90 × 60
k 30 × 700
l 60 × 60
m 400 × 30
n 600 × 80
o 80 × 90

2 Work out the answer to each calculation mentally.

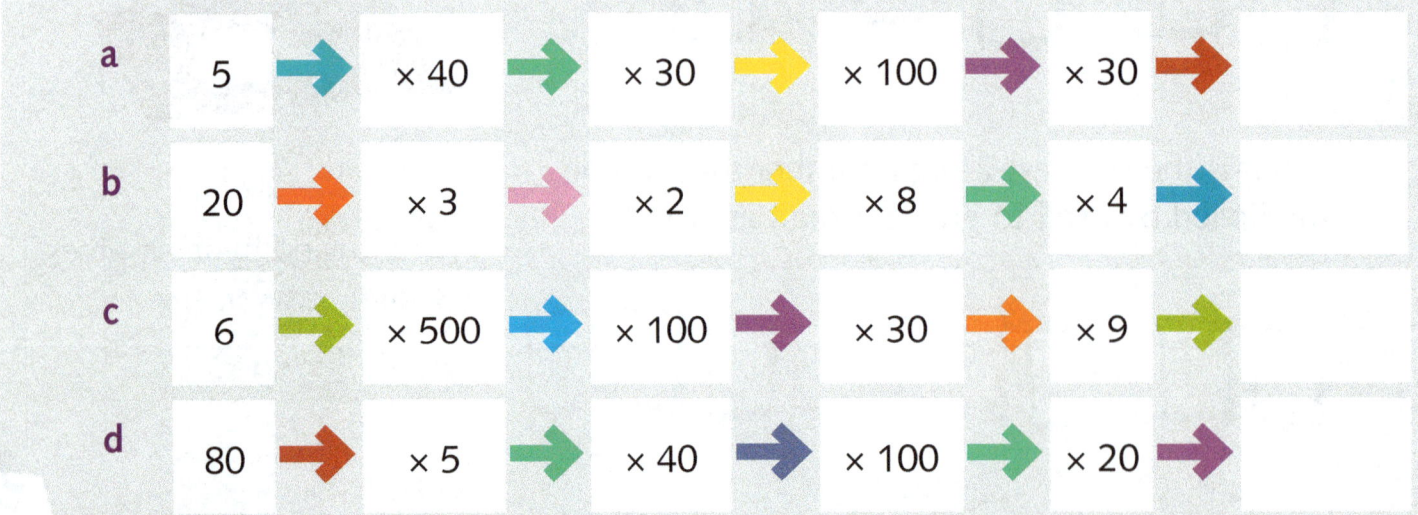

a 5 → × 40 → × 30 → × 100 → × 30 →
b 20 → × 3 → × 2 → × 8 → × 4 →
c 6 → × 500 → × 100 → × 30 → × 9 →
d 80 → × 5 → × 40 → × 100 → × 20 →

Challenge 2

Estimate the answer to each calculation. Find the answer using the expanded written method. Then compare your answer with your estimate.

Example

$537 \times 33 \rightarrow 500 \times 30 = 15\,000$

		5	3	7	
×			3	3	
	1	6¹	1²	1	(537 × 3)
1	6¹	1²	1	0	(537 × 30)
1	7	7	2	1	

		5	3	7	
×			3	3	
1	6¹	1²	1	0	(537 × 30)
	1	6¹	1²	1	(537 × 3)
1	7	7	2	1	

a 536 × 52
b 149 × 43
c 278 × 37
d 418 × 15
e 527 × 39
f 614 × 78
g 778 × 76
h 546 × 63
i 479 × 69

Challenge 3

Find the answers to these problems.

a For every 8 people buying a train ticket, 1 person goes free. A group of 64 people buy train tickets to Paris. The price per person for the journey is €483. How much money do they spend on tickets altogether?

b If a plane travels at 506 kilometres per hour, how far will it travel in 13 hours? How far would it travel in one day? Suggest possible destinations it might travel to and from in these times.

c Sebastian uses his car for business travel. On average he travels 678 km per week. How many kilometres does he travel in a year? Write a statement to justify your answer.

33

Unit 6, Week 1, Lesson 4

Multiplication HTO × TO using the formal written method

- Use the formal written method of long multiplication to calculate HTO × TO
- Estimate and check the answer to a calculation

Challenge 1

1. Round these numbers to the nearest 10.

   | 64 | 38 | 89 | 179 | 654 | 327 | 793 |

2. Round these numbers to the nearest 100.

   | 415 | 625 | 811 | 557 | 478 | 762 | 899 |

3. Work these calculations out mentally.

   a) 360 × 8
   b) 430 × 6
   c) 570 × 4
   d) 820 × 9
   e) 57 × 80
   f) 64 × 30
   g) 35 × 70
   h) 98 × 50

34

Challenge 2

1 Estimate the answer to each calculation.
Find the answer using the formal written method.
Then compare your answer with your estimate.

Example

246 × 38 → 200 × 40 = 8 000

Th	H	T	O
		2	4	6
×			3	8
1	9³	6⁴	8
7¹	3¹	8	0
9	3	4	8
	1	1	

Th	H	T	O
		2	4	6
×			3	8
7¹	3¹	8	0
1	9³	6⁴	8
9	3	4	8
	1	1	

a 462 × 35
b 413 × 49
c 258 × 51
d 628 × 25
e 247 × 69
f 314 × 86
g 888 × 88
h 546 × 78
i 666 × 77

2 Five of these calculations have the same answer. Can you find them?

238 × 72   453 × 42   952 × 18   4194 × 4   378 × 52
476 × 36   2832 × 6   1904 × 9   376 × 46   4284 × 4

Challenge 3

Find the missing digits in these calculations.

a
```
      2 ☐ 9
    ×   ☐ 7
    ─────────
      ☐ ☐ 3 ☐
    ☐ ☐ 7 ☐
    ─────────
      8 1 0 ☐
```

b
```
      3 6 5
    ×   ☐ ☐
    ─────────
      2 9 2 0
    7 3 0 0
    ─────────
    ☐ ☐ ☐ ☐ ☐
```

c
```
      ☐ ☐ ☐
    ×   6 9
    ─────────
      3 6 5 4
    2 4 3 6 0
    ─────────
    ☐ ☐ ☐ ☐ ☐
```

35

Unit 6, Week 2, Lesson 1

Multiplying decimals using mental methods

Use mental methods to multiply a decimal by a whole number

Challenge 1

1 How many tenths does each of these numbers represent?

Example
2·7 = 27 tenths

3·6 8·4 7 6·8 4·2 8·9 25

2 How many hundredths does each of these numbers represent?

Example
2·5 = 250 hundredths

5·36 0·62 3·1 4·53 0·02 2·34 7

Challenge 2

Fill in the missing numbers to make the calculations complete.

a ★ × 4 = 1·2   b ■ × 6 = 0·36   c ★ × 7 = 2·8
d ■ × 5 = 0·05   e ★ × 8 = 6·4   f 6 × ■ = 2·4
g 9 × ★ = 0·45   h 8 × ■ = 4·0   i 3·6 = ★ × 4
j ■ × 7 = 5·6   k 6·8 × 7 = ★   l ■ = 4 × 0·78
m 7·4 × 8 = ★   n 9·6 × 5 = ■   o 0·47 × 6 = ★

36

Challenge 3

Find the related calculations. Write them as a set.
Find the answer to each one.

Example

$6 \times 8 = 48$
$0.6 \times 8 = 4.8$
$0.06 \times 8 = 0.48$

0·73 × 8	4·6 × 4	73 × 8	7·9 × 6	6·4 × 6
5·8 × 7	46 × 4	64 × 9	0·87 × 3	79 × 6
0·64 × 9	8·7 × 3	0·45 × 8	8·1 × 6	87 × 3
81 × 6	4·5 × 8	2·2 × 1	7·3 × 8	22 × 1
58 × 7	0·64 × 6	0·46 × 4	6·4 × 9	0·81 × 6
45 × 8	64 × 6	0·79 × 6	0·22 × 1	0·58 × 7

Unit 6, Week 2, Lesson 2

Multiplying decimals by a 1-digit number using the grid method

- Multiply a decimal by a 1-digit number using the grid method
- Estimate and check the answer to a calculation

Challenge 1

1 For each machine work out the output number for each input number.

a ×3
 6
 0·1
 0·07
 4
 0·9

b ×8
 0·04
 6
 0·8
 0·07
 0·9

c ×6
 9
 0·08
 0·07
 0·4
 0·02

2 Dylan answered each of these calculations incorrectly. Copy each calculation writing the correct answer.

a 0·7 × 5 = 35 ✗

b 0·8 × 3 = 0·24 ✗

c 0·03 × 4 = 1·2 ✗

d 0·8 × 9 = 0·72 ✗

e 0·02 × 7 = 1·4 ✗

f 0·8 × 4 = 32 ✗

g 0·5 × 5 = 0·25 ✗

h 0·09 × 7 = 6·3 ✗

i 0·6 × 9 = 5·04 ✗

j 0·04 × 3 = 12 ✗

k 0·6 × 6 = 0·36 ✗

l 0·03 × 8 = 0·024 ✗

Challenge 2

Estimate the answer to each calculation. Find the answer using the grid method. Then compare your answer with your estimate.

Example

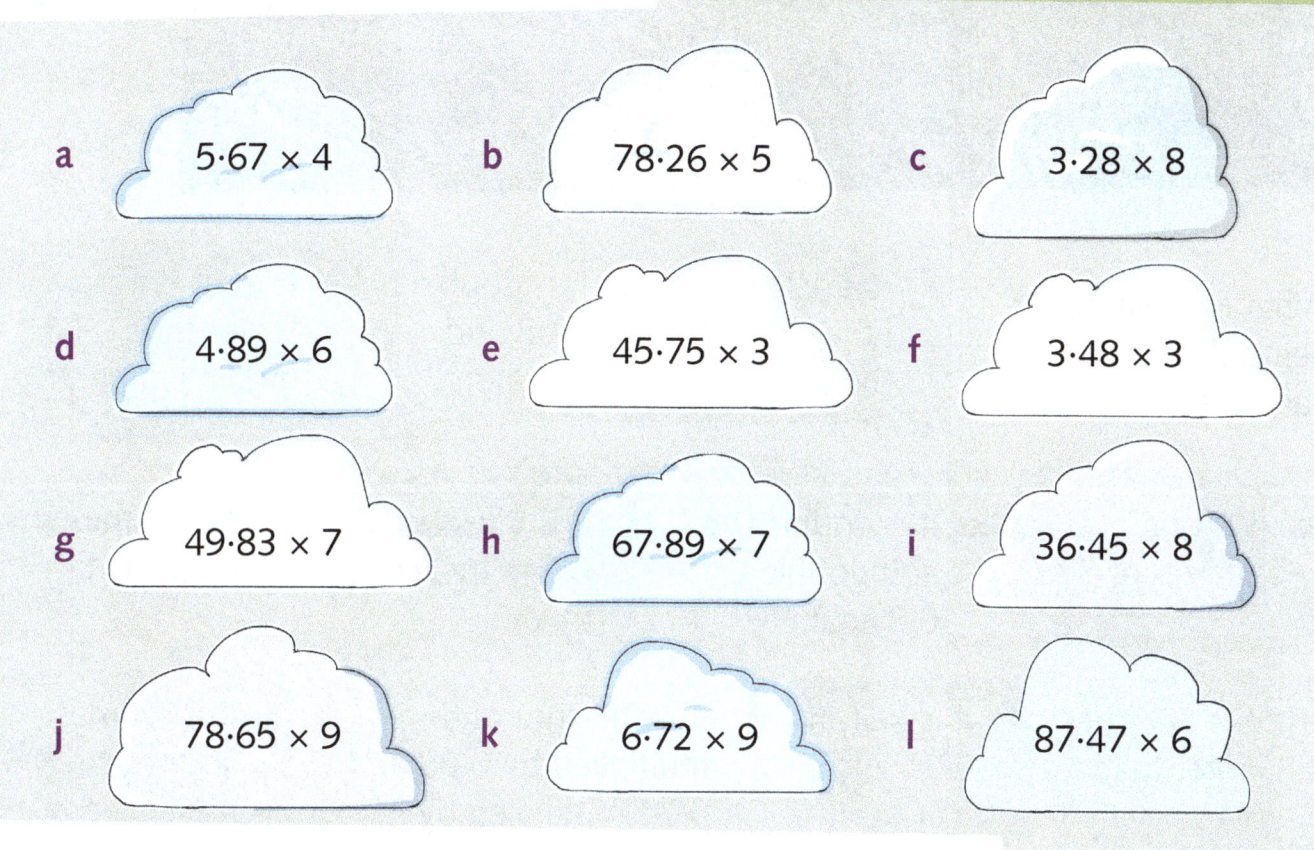

36·74 × 6 → 40 × 6 = 240

×	30	6	0·7	0·04
6	180	36	4·2	0·24	= 220·44

a) 5·67 × 4
b) 78·26 × 5
c) 3·28 × 8
d) 4·89 × 6
e) 45·75 × 3
f) 3·48 × 3
g) 49·83 × 7
h) 67·89 × 7
i) 36·45 × 8
j) 78·65 × 9
k) 6·72 × 9
l) 87·47 × 6

Challenge 3

Play this game with a partner. Take turns to:

- choose a number from below (you can only choose each number once)
- roll the dice
- multiply the number on the dice by your chosen number.

Choose the most appropriate method to calculate the answer, mental or written. If you choose a written method, write the approximate answer first and then show your working out. The person with the highest answer scores one point. The first person to score ten points is the winner.

You will need:
- 0–9 or 1–10 dice

44·56   31·3   6·24   9·43   8·68   49·9   7·85   36·1   25·24   13·3

Unit 6, Week 2, Lesson 3

Multiplying decimals by a 1-digit number using the expanded written method

- Multiply a decimal by a 1-digit number using the expanded written method of short multiplication
- Estimate and check the answer to a calculation

Challenge 1

What is the number being described in each clue?

a It is 12 times larger than 0·4.

b It is double 0·08 and 0·4 more.

c It is 20 times larger than 0·03 multiplied by 2.

d It is one quarter of 32.

e It is double 0·8 and double 0·8 again.

f It is 5 less than 25 multiplied by 0·5.

g It is 5 times more than 4·9.

h It is 10 times larger than 0·15.

i It is half of 0·64 and half again.

j It is the sum of 4 multiplied by 0·08 and 0·24 multiplied by 4.

k It is 4 times larger than 0·3 multiplied by 3.

Challenge 2

Find the answer to these calculations using the expanded written method of short multiplication.

Estimate the answer first. Convert the decimals to whole numbers, carry out the calculation, then convert the answer back to a decimal.

a 2·78 × 5
b 4·35 × 4
c 6·74 × 3
d 65·78 × 6
e 36·74 × 8
f 38·76 × 5
g 83·45 × 9
h 2·78 × 5
i 76·38 × 4
j 6·74 × 7

Example

4·63 × 8 → 5 × 8 = 40

	4	6	3	
×			8	
		2	4	(3 × 8)
	4	8	0	(60 × 8)
3	2	0	0	(400 × 8)
3	7	0	4	
	1			

4·63 × 8 is equivalent to 463 × 8 ÷ 100. This equals 3704 ÷ 100, which is 37·04.

4·63 × 8 = 37·04

40

Challenge 3

1 Work out the total cost of each purchase. Write your answer in euros (€).

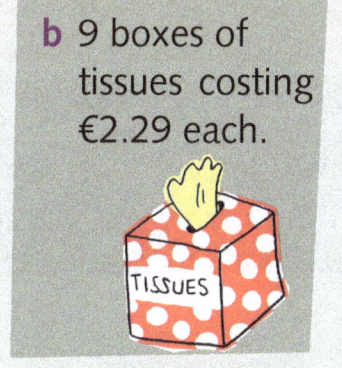

a 3 boxes of eggs costing €3.89 each.

b 9 boxes of tissues costing €2.29 each.

c 6 boxes of chocolates costing €5.68 each.

d 8 pizzas costing €6.89 each.

e 6 sandwiches costing €4.50 each.

f 5 pencils costing €1.76 each.

g 7 loaves of bread costing €2.49.

h 7 milkshakes costing €2.44 each.

2 Work out the total cost of each purchase. Write your answer in euros (€).

a 8 jumpers costing €89.65 each.

b 6 candles costing €25.90 each.

c 4 kettles costing €63.50 each.

d 9 photo frames costing €43.90 each.

e 4 bunches of flowers costing €17.96 each.

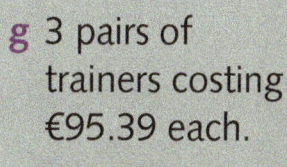

f 5 watches costing €84.55 each.

g 3 pairs of trainers costing €95.39 each.

h 5 footballs costing €12.27 each.

Unit 6, Week 2, Lesson 4

Multiplying decimals by a 1-digit number using the formal written method

- Multiply a decimal by a 1-digit number using the formal written method of short multiplication
- Estimate and check the answer to a calculation

Challenge 1

1 Work out these calculations.

a	6 × 3	b	7 × 8	c	9 × 6	d	4 × 7
	0·6 × 3		0·7 × 8		0·9 × 6		4 × 0·7
	0·06 × 3		0·07 × 8		0·09 × 6		4 × 0·07
e	8 × 9	f	3 × 4	g	9 × 7	h	8 × 6
	0·8 × 9		3 × 0·4		9 × 0·7		0·8 × 6
	0·08 × 9		3 × 0·04		9 × 0.07		0.08 × 6

2 Write the answer to each multiplication chain.

a 0·2 → × 4 → × 6 →

b 0·05 → × 8 → × 9 →

c 0·9 → × 4 → × 2 →

d 0·2 → × 5 → × 40 →

e 0·06 → × 3 → × 4 →

f 0·7 → × 9 → × 7 →

Challenge 2

Find the answer to these calculations using the formal written method of short multiplication.

Estimate the answer first. Convert the decimals to whole numbers, carry out the calculation, then convert the answer back to a decimal.

a 33·3 × 8
b 6·73 × 3
c 27·3 × 9
d 2·78 × 7
e 76·54 × 6
f 8·94 × 6
g 67·25 × 4
h 38·29 × 5
i 9·86 × 7

Example

71·4 × 7 → 70 × 7 = 490

Th	H	T	O
	7	1	4
×		²	7
4	9	9	8

71·4 × 7 is equivalent to 714 × 7 ÷ 10. This equals 4998 ÷ 10, which is 499·8.

71·4 × 7 = 499·8

Challenge 3

Find the answers to these problems.

a Keira buys 5 paperback books each costing €6.85. She pays with a €50 note. How much change does she receive?

b Mahdi bought 5 hardback books each costing €18.50. How much more did Mahdi spend than Keira on books?

c Rosie has €50 to spend. She prefers magazines to books. On holiday she buys 1 magazine each day for a week. Each magazine costs €3.80. How much money does she have left?

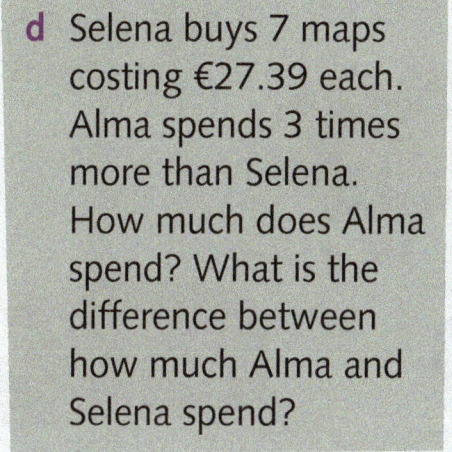

d Selena buys 7 maps costing €27.39 each. Alma spends 3 times more than Selena. How much does Alma spend? What is the difference between how much Alma and Selena spend?

e The cost for travelling in Tina's taxi is 9 cents per 100m. Sonya travels 15.62 km. How much does she pay?

43

Unit 6, Week 3, Lesson 1

Mass in action

Convert between grams and kilograms using decimals to 3 places

Challenge 1

1 Write each mass using decimal notation.

a i $\frac{3}{10}$ kg   ii $\frac{3}{100}$ kg   iii $\frac{3}{1000}$ kg

b i $\frac{7}{10}$ kg   ii $\frac{7}{100}$ kg   iii $\frac{7}{1000}$ kg

Example

$\frac{1}{10}$ kg = 0·1 kg

$\frac{1}{100}$ kg = 0·01 kg

$\frac{1}{1000}$ kg = 0·001 kg

2 Convert each mass to kilograms using decimal notation.

a i 400 g   ii 40 g   iii 4 g

b i 900 g   ii 90 g   iii 9 g

c i 1200 g   ii 120 g   iii 12 g

Example

100 g = 0·1 kg
10 g = 0·01 kg
1 g   = 0·001 kg

3 Convert each mass to grams.

a i 0·8 kg   ii 0·08 kg   iii 0·008 kg

b i 4·5 kg   ii 4·05 kg   iii 4·005 kg

Example

1.03 kg = 1030 g

Challenge 2

1 Convert the mass of each sports bag to kilograms then round your answer to one decimal place.

Example

4545 g = 4·545 kg
       = 4·5 kg

a 6818 g    b 9090 g     c 7366 g

d 14 275 g   e 12 050 g    f 10 025 g

44

2 Calculate the total mass of each pair of parcels in kilograms then convert your answer to grams.

Example

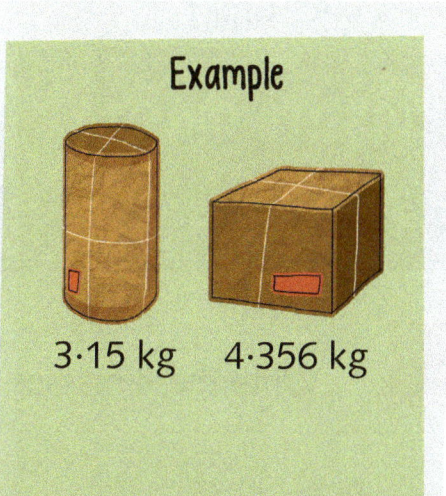

3·15 kg   4·356 kg

3·15 + 4·356 = 7·506 kg
7·506 kg = 7506 g

a 3·4 kg   4·56 kg

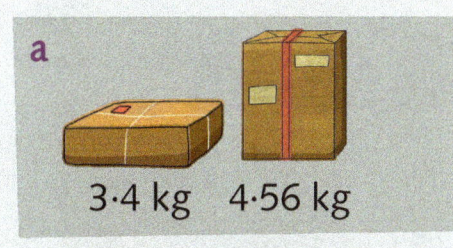

b 6·17 kg   5·8 kg

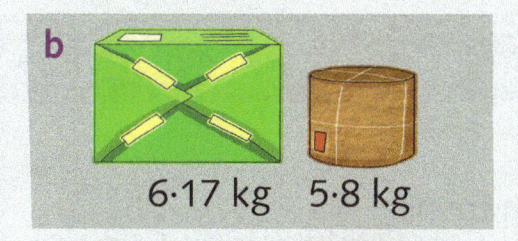

c 7·52 kg   9·375 kg

d 4·27 kg   8·135 kg

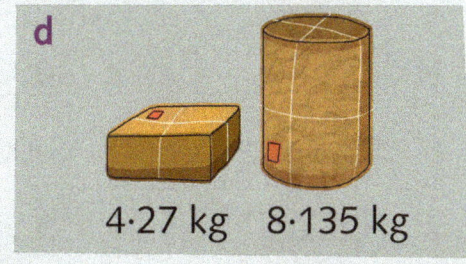

e 8·245 kg   4·606 kg

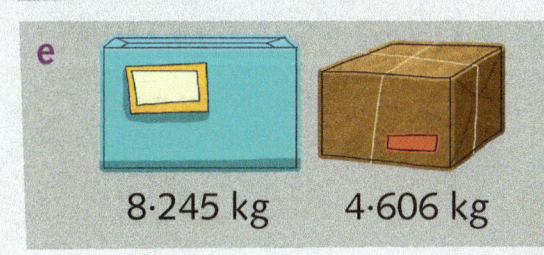

f 10·875 kg   9·125 kg

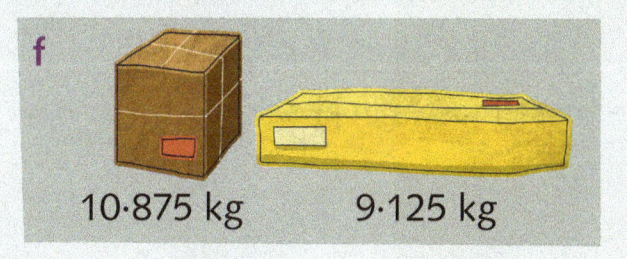

Challenge 3

Every Euro coin of the same value has exactly the same mass when it is put into circulation by the central banks.

€2 coin: 8·5 g
€1 coin: 7·5 g 
50c coin: 7·8 g 
20c coin: 5·75 g 
10c coin: 4·1 g 
5c coin: 3·92 g 
2c coin: 3·06 g 
1c coin: 2·3 g 

1 Find in grams and then in kilograms the total mass of 100 coins of each denomination of coin.

2 Calculate the total value of:

a 1·5 kg of €1 coins
b 4·6 kg of 1c coins
c 0·918 kg of 2c coins
d 1·56 kg of 50c coins

45

Unit 6, Week 3, Lesson 2

Massive masses

Convert between kilograms and tonnes using decimals to 3 places

Challenge 1

1 Write these masses in tonnes.

a 6000 kg
b 9000 kg
c 3000 kg
d 12 000 kg
e 5700 kg
f 6800 kg
g 13 600 kg
h 21 700 kg
i 19 900 kg

Example

2000 kg = 2 t
2700 kg = 2·7 t

2 Write these masses in kilograms.

a 1·4 t
b 3·8 t
c 7·9 t
d 15·5 t
e 18·7 t
f 24·6 t

Example

5·3 t = 5300 kg

Challenge 2

1 Copy and complete the table, which shows the average mass of adult whales.

Whale	Tonnes (t)	Kilograms (kg)
blue	150	150 000
bowhead	100	
sei		20 000
humpback	30	
grey	28·5	
minke		7500
bottlenose	6·5	
killer		3988
pilot		2200
narwhal		1250

46

2 How many times heavier is the blue whale than:

   a the humpback whale?   b the minke whale?

3 How many times heavier is the bowhead whale than the sei whale?

4 What is the approximate total mass in tonnes of a pod of:

   a 8 narwhals?   b 5 pilot whales?   c 10 killer whales?

5 The average mass of an adult African elephant is 4800 kg. How many elephants will have a total mass to the nearest tonne as that of 1 grey whale to the nearest tonne?

Challenge 3

1 Calculate in kilograms:

   a the mass of krill that a blue whale eats in one day.

   b the difference between the average and the heaviest recorded mass of the blue whale.

2 What is the approximate mass of a baby blue whale:

   a at 10 days old?

   b at 10 weeks old?

3 The mass of a slice of pizza is 0·2 kg. How many times larger would the pizza slice have to be to match the daily appetite of an average blue whale?

Facts about blue whales

- They are the largest living creatures on Earth.
- They have an average mass of 150 tonnes.
- The heaviest ever caught had a mass of about 190 tonnes.
- Their daily consumption of krill, small sea creatures similar to shrimp, is about 4 tonnes.
- At birth the mass of a baby blue whale is about 3000 kg.
- A baby blue whale will gain about 100 kg in mass each day.

Unit 6, Week 3, Lesson 3

Backpack masses

Convert between grams and kilograms to solve problems

Oscar: 5·248 kg

Mina: 5·813 kg

Terry: 6·478 kg

Julie: 4·685 kg

Steve: 8·157 kg

Abby: 7·589 kg

Challenge 1

1 Write the mass of each backpack in grams.

2 Write the number of grams represented by the number 8 in the mass of each child's backpack.

3 Find the difference in kilograms between the backpacks of Oscar and Steve.

Challenge 2

1 Round the mass of each backpack to the nearest tenth of one kilogram and then to the nearest kilogram. Record your results in a table.

Backpack	Rounded to nearest $\frac{1}{10}$ kg (kg)	Rounded to nearest kg (kg)
Oscar	5·2	5
Mina		
Terry		
Julie		
Steve		
Abby		

2 All 6 backpacks were loaded into the back of the minivan. Use the answers in your table for Question 1 to calculate the total mass of the 6 backpacks to the nearest kilogram.

3 Find the difference in grams between the backpacks of these children.

   a Oscar and Terry   b Mina and Steve   c Julie and Abby

4 Which three backpacks have the same combined mass as the combined mass of Steve's and Abby's backpacks?

5 Use the pictures below to answer the questions.

a For each of the fruits, find the approximate mass of:

   i 1 fruit in grams   ii 10 fruits in kilograms   iii 100 fruits in kilograms

b Mina put 2 apples and 1 banana into her lunch box. What was the total mass of her fruit in kilograms?

Challenge 3

Three spaniel puppies have a combined mass of 11·9 kg.

- Harry is 0·4 kg heavier than Holly.
- Holly is 200 g heavier than Heather.

What is the mass of each puppy in kilograms?

Unit 6, Week 3, Lesson 4

Newspaper problems

Convert between grams and kilograms to solve problems

This tables gives the mass of one copy of four daily newspapers and two Sunday newspapers.

Newspaper	Echo	Express	Globe	Times	Post on Sunday	Sunday News
Mass (g)	275	310	250	400	400	500

Challenge 1

Copy and complete the table showing the mass in kilograms for 1, 10 and 100 copies of each of the daily newspapers.

Number of copies	Echo	Express	Globe	Times
1	0·275 kg	0·31 kg	0·25 kg	0·4 kg
10	2·75 kg			
100				

Challenge 2

1 Work out the mass in grams then in kilograms for each number of copies of the daily newspapers. Copy and complete the table below.

Newspaper	Number of copies	Total mass (g)	Total mass (kg)
Echo	20		
Express	50		
Globe	40		
Times	30		

50

2 Calculate the mass in kilograms of newspapers delivered to each house in one week.

	Address	Daily (Mon–Sat)	Sunday
a	6 Ash Avenue	Express	Sunday News
b	10 Oak Grove	Times	Post on Sunday
c	35 Rowan Road	Globe	Post on Sunday
d	15 Willow Way	Echo, Times	Sunday News

3 The newspapers in Zac's bag at the start of his paper round each day have a mass of 7·385 kg. He has 5 copies of the Echo, 6 copies of the Express and 7 copies of the Globe. The rest of his newspapers are copies of the Times.

   a How many copies of the Times does he have in his bag?

   b What is the total mass in kilograms of the daily newspapers he delivers from Monday to Saturday?

4 Alfie delivers 17 copies of the Post on Sunday and 13 copies of the Sunday News to 20 houses. What is the total mass in kilograms of his newspapers at the start of his Sunday paper round?

5 How much heavier is Alfie's set of Sunday newspapers than Zac's set of daily newspapers?

6 How many of Alfie's customers take two Sunday newspapers?

Challenge 3

1 Grace, David and Lauren each have a newspaper round. The combined mass of newspapers in their bags is 21 kg. Grace's newspapers are 600 g lighter than David's newspapers. David and Lauren have exactly the same mass of newspapers. What is the mass of each child's newspapers?

2 Make up a similar newspaper-related problem for a partner to solve.

Unit 7, Week 1, Lesson 1

Adding and subtracting fractions (1)

Add and subtract fractions with different denominators and mixed numbers, using the concept of equivalent fractions

Challenge 1

1. Work out each of these fraction addition and subtraction calculations. Remember to start by changing both fractions to equivalent fractions with the same denominator.

Example

$$\frac{3}{5} - \frac{1}{2} = \frac{6}{10} - \frac{5}{10} = \frac{1}{10}$$

10 is a multiple of 5 and 2, so I can change them both to tenths.

a $\frac{3}{4} + \frac{1}{2}$
b $\frac{2}{5} + \frac{4}{10}$
c $\frac{4}{6} + \frac{5}{12}$
d $\frac{2}{3} + \frac{4}{6}$
e $\frac{7}{12} + \frac{1}{6}$

f $\frac{8}{14} + \frac{3}{7}$
g $\frac{1}{4} + \frac{3}{5}$
h $\frac{3}{6} + \frac{4}{9}$
i $\frac{1}{2} + \frac{2}{3}$
j $\frac{4}{5} + \frac{1}{2}$

k $\frac{3}{4} - \frac{1}{2}$
l $\frac{4}{5} - \frac{3}{10}$
m $\frac{2}{3} - \frac{2}{6}$
n $\frac{9}{12} - \frac{3}{6}$
o $\frac{11}{14} - \frac{4}{7}$

p $\frac{3}{4} - \frac{2}{5}$
q $\frac{5}{6} - \frac{2}{9}$
r $\frac{1}{2} - \frac{1}{3}$
s $\frac{3}{5} - \frac{1}{2}$
t $\frac{5}{8} - \frac{1}{3}$

2. Look at your answers to Question 1. If any of them are improper fractions, write them as mixed numbers.

Challenge 2

1. Work out each of these mixed number calculations. Write each answer as a whole number and a proper fraction.

   a $12\frac{3}{4} + 11\frac{4}{5}$ b $17\frac{4}{10} + 9\frac{3}{4}$ c $18\frac{2}{8} + 16\frac{7}{12}$ d $27\frac{7}{9} + 25\frac{4}{6}$

   e $21\frac{2}{6} + 18\frac{3}{4}$ f $29\frac{5}{7} + 22\frac{3}{5}$ g $24\frac{12}{15} + 26\frac{4}{10}$ h $31\frac{3}{5} + 24\frac{4}{6}$

   i $22\frac{3}{6} + 38\frac{5}{7}$ j $27\frac{3}{8} + 41\frac{1}{5}$ k $26\frac{3}{4} - 14\frac{2}{5}$ l $28\frac{9}{10} - 19\frac{3}{4}$

   m $29\frac{5}{8} - 21\frac{5}{6}$ n $32\frac{3}{4} - 25\frac{2}{6}$ o $39\frac{3}{7} - 29\frac{4}{5}$ p $33\frac{2}{10} - 20\frac{8}{15}$

2. Sam has worked out the calculation on the white board incorrectly. How do you think he worked it out? What do you think he does not understand? Work out the answer correctly to make sure.

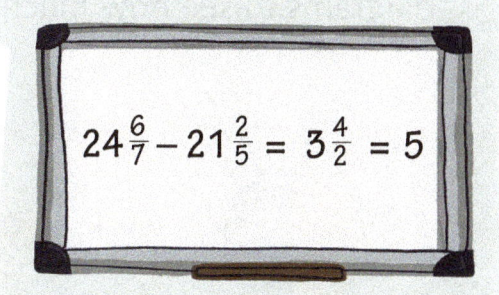

   $24\frac{6}{7} - 21\frac{2}{5} = 3\frac{4}{2} = 5$

3. The tea urn in the school staffroom gets filled to the top every morning. It holds 6 litres of water. Each cup of tea or coffee uses $\frac{1}{20}$ of the water.

   - At playtime, 7 people have a cup of coffee and 2 have a cup of tea.
   - Then a teacher comes to fill a water jug with hot water. This uses up $\frac{1}{5}$ of the amount of water that was in the urn to start with.
   - At lunchtime a teacher uses some hot water to make her soup. This uses up $\frac{1}{10}$ of a full urn.

   What fraction of the water is now left in the urn?

Challenge 3

Copy and complete these addition fractions walls. Always write your answers as mixed numbers.

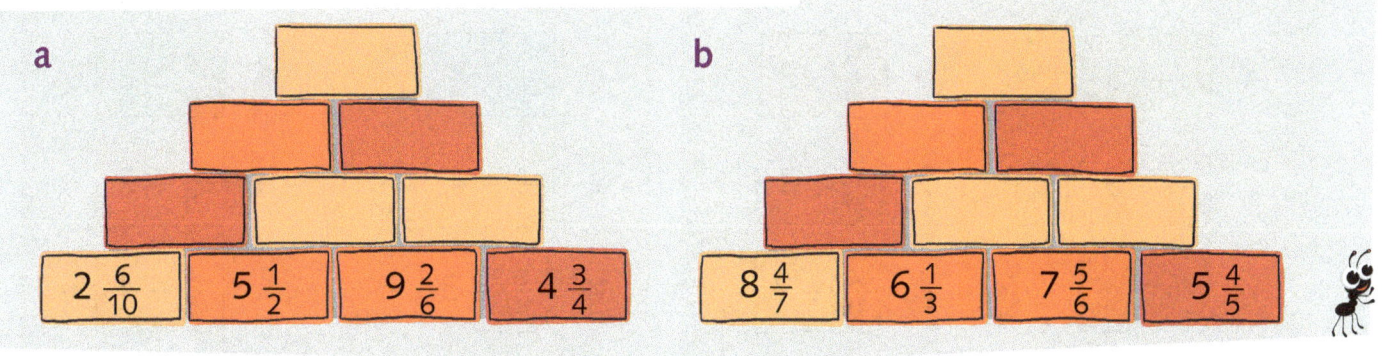

a $2\frac{6}{10}$ $5\frac{1}{2}$ $9\frac{2}{6}$ $4\frac{3}{4}$

b $8\frac{4}{7}$ $6\frac{1}{3}$ $7\frac{5}{6}$ $5\frac{4}{5}$

Unit 7, Week 1, Lesson 2

Dividing fractions

Divide proper fractions by whole numbers

Example

$\frac{1}{2} \div 4 = \frac{1}{8}$

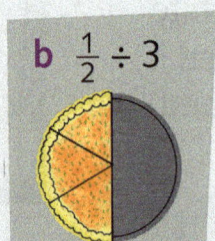

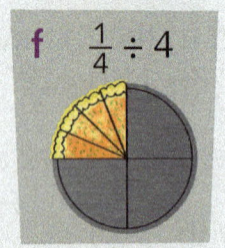

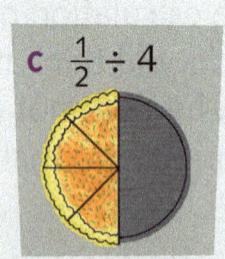

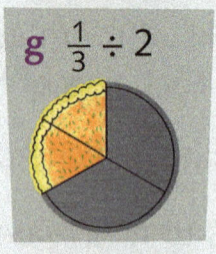

Challenge 1

In this question the fractions are represented as pizzas. Divide the fractions by the whole numbers and use the diagrams to see how much each person gets.

a $\frac{1}{2} \div 2$ 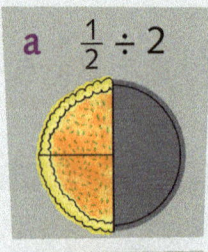
b $\frac{1}{2} \div 3$
c $\frac{1}{2} \div 4$
d $\frac{1}{4} \div 2$

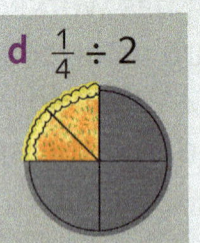

e $\frac{1}{4} \div 3$ 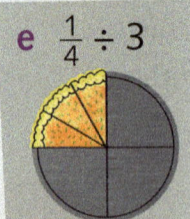
f $\frac{1}{4} \div 4$
g $\frac{1}{3} \div 2$
h $\frac{1}{3} \div 3$

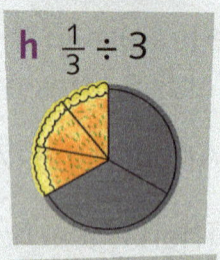

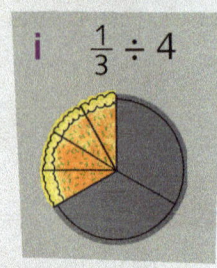

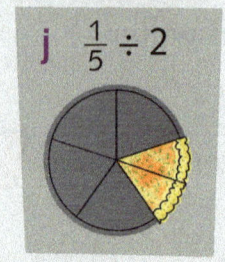

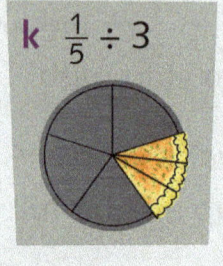

i $\frac{1}{3} \div 4$
j $\frac{1}{5} \div 2$
k $\frac{1}{5} \div 3$
l $\frac{1}{5} \div 4$

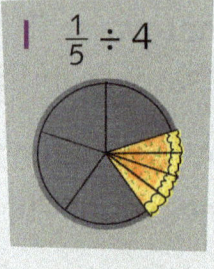

Challenge 2

1 Work out these fraction divisions. Give each answer in its simplest form.

Example

$\frac{2}{5} \div 4 = \frac{2}{20} = \frac{1}{10}$

a $\frac{2}{3} \div 3$
b $\frac{2}{5} \div 2$
c $\frac{3}{5} \div 3$
d $\frac{4}{6} \div 2$

e $\frac{2}{6} \div 3$
f $\frac{3}{4} \div 3$
g $\frac{3}{4} \div 4$
h $\frac{2}{8} \div 2$

i $\frac{5}{8} \div 3$
j $\frac{4}{10} \div 2$
k $\frac{6}{10} \div 3$
l $\frac{4}{5} \div 4$

2 Answer these word problems.

  a Lucas the chef uses $\frac{2}{3}$ kg of flour to bake 4 cakes.
     What weight of flour does he use to bake each cake?

  b Lucas uses $\frac{3}{5}$ of a bag of icing sugar to ice his 4 cakes.
     How much of the bag of icing sugar does he use to ice each cake?

  c Lucas uses $\frac{1}{6}$ of a bag of sprinkles to decorate the 4 cakes.
     How much of the bag of sprinkles does he use to decorate each cake?

3 Think of a time when you and your family or friends have shared something that was less than one whole. Draw a diagram and write the fraction division to go with it.

Challenge 3

1 Explain why the method for dividing fractions works. Use diagrams as part of your explanation.

2 Work out these fraction divisions. Give each answer in its simplest form.

  a $\frac{5}{8} \div 6$ b $\frac{4}{7} \div 5$ c $\frac{3}{4} \div 7$ d $\frac{6}{9} \div 5$

  e $\frac{8}{10} \div 6$ f $\frac{7}{11} \div 4$ g $\frac{9}{12} \div 5$ h $\frac{2}{8} \div 6$

  i $\frac{4}{10} \div 6$ j $\frac{3}{9} \div 6$ k $\frac{8}{13} \div 4$ l $\frac{10}{15} \div 6$

  m $\frac{4}{10} \div 5$ n $\frac{7}{11} \div 4$ o $\frac{3}{8} \div 3$ p $\frac{6}{14} \div 7$

3 Divide this fraction by five different whole numbers. $\boxed{\frac{8}{10}}$

4 Choose four calculations from Question 2 and write a word problem to go with each of them.

Unit 7, Week 1, Lesson 3

Multiplying fractions

Multiply simple pairs of proper fractions, writing the answer in its simplest form

Challenge 1

1 Work out the following multiplication calculations.

a $\quad \dfrac{1}{2} \times \dfrac{1}{3} = \dfrac{1 \times 1}{2 \times 3} = \dfrac{\Box}{\Box}$

b $\quad \dfrac{1}{5} \times \dfrac{1}{2} = \dfrac{1 \times 1}{5 \times 2} = \dfrac{\Box}{\Box}$

c $\quad \dfrac{1}{3} \times \dfrac{1}{2} = \dfrac{1 \times 1}{\Box \times \Box} = \dfrac{\Box}{\Box}$

d $\quad \dfrac{1}{4} \times \dfrac{1}{3} = \dfrac{1 \times 1}{\Box \times \Box} = \dfrac{\Box}{\Box}$

e $\quad \dfrac{1}{6} \times \dfrac{1}{2} = \dfrac{1 \times 1}{\Box \times \Box} = \dfrac{\Box}{\Box}$

f $\quad \dfrac{1}{3} \times \dfrac{1}{4} = \dfrac{1 \times 1}{\Box \times \Box} = \dfrac{\Box}{\Box}$

g $\quad \dfrac{1}{5} \times \dfrac{1}{3} = \dfrac{1 \times 1}{\Box \times \Box} = \dfrac{\Box}{\Box}$

h $\quad \dfrac{1}{4} \times \dfrac{1}{2} = \dfrac{1 \times 1}{\Box \times \Box} = \dfrac{\Box}{\Box}$

2 Work out the following multiplication calculations and give each answer in its simplest form.

a $\quad \dfrac{2}{3} \times \dfrac{1}{4} = \dfrac{2 \times 1}{\Box \times \Box} = \dfrac{\Box}{\Box}$

b $\quad \dfrac{2}{5} \times \dfrac{1}{2} = \dfrac{2 \times 1}{\Box \times \Box} = \dfrac{\Box}{\Box}$

c $\quad \dfrac{1}{3} \times \dfrac{2}{6} = \dfrac{1 \times 2}{\Box \times \Box} = \dfrac{\Box}{\Box}$

d $\quad \dfrac{2}{4} \times \dfrac{2}{5} = \dfrac{2 \times 2}{\Box \times \Box} = \dfrac{\Box}{\Box}$

e $\quad \dfrac{3}{4} \times \dfrac{2}{3} = \dfrac{3 \times 2}{\Box \times \Box} = \dfrac{\Box}{\Box}$

f $\quad \dfrac{4}{5} \times \dfrac{3}{4} = \dfrac{4 \times 3}{\Box \times \Box} = \dfrac{\Box}{\Box}$

Challenge 2

1 Choose 10 different pairs of fractions from below to multiply together. Work out the answer to each fraction multiplication calculation, writing your answer in its simplest form.

Example

$$\frac{2}{3} \times \frac{1}{6} = \frac{2 \times 1}{3 \times 6} = \frac{2}{18} = \frac{1}{9}$$

Fractions on stars: $\frac{2}{3}$, $\frac{4}{5}$, $\frac{3}{5}$, $\frac{1}{5}$, $\frac{1}{2}$, $\frac{2}{6}$, $\frac{2}{8}$, $\frac{1}{4}$, $\frac{4}{6}$, $\frac{3}{7}$, $\frac{5}{8}$, $\frac{3}{9}$, $\frac{3}{4}$, $\frac{2}{10}$, $\frac{1}{3}$, $\frac{1}{6}$

2 Choose one of the fraction multiplication calculations that you wrote in Question 1 and use it to write an explanation as to how to multiply pairs of fractions. Show your explanation to a partner and ask them to suggest how you might improve it.

Challenge 3

Play this game with a partner.

- Both players roll the dice four times and record the digits. 0 counts as 10.
- Use your four digits to make a fraction multiplication, like this: ☐/☐ × ☐/☐
- If the denominator of your answer is on the fraction wall on Resource 77: Fraction wall (2), you can colour in the appropriate number of sections on your sheet.
- Have 10 turns each.
- Work out the total fraction of the fraction wall you have coloured in.
- The winner is the player who has coloured in the most.

You will need:
- copies of Resource 77: Fraction wall (2)
- 0–9 dice
- coloured pencil

My fraction multiplication was:

$$\frac{6}{8} \times \frac{2}{4} = \frac{12}{32} = \frac{3}{8}$$

I can colour in three $\frac{1}{8}$ sections on the fraction wall.

57

Unit 7, Week 1, Lesson 4

Fraction problems

Solve problems involving fractions

You will need:
- 1–6 dice

Example

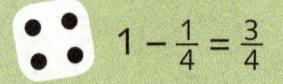

$1 - \frac{1}{4} = \frac{3}{4}$

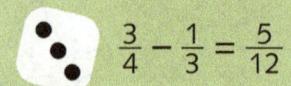

$\frac{3}{4} - \frac{1}{3} = \frac{5}{12}$

$\frac{5}{12} - \frac{1}{5} = \frac{13}{60}$

$\frac{13}{60}$ is less than $\frac{1}{4}$

Challenge 1

1. Work out how much pie is left. Start with one whole pie.
   - Roll the dice and read the number as a unit fraction. This will be the amount of pie that will be eaten. Roll again if you roll a 1.
   - Write the subtraction calculation to work out what fraction of the pie is left.
   - Repeat until there is less than $\frac{1}{4}$ of the pie left. Do this for three pies.

2. These ingredients are for 1 apple pie. The chef wants to cook 2 pies. Work out how much of each ingredient she needs.

Apple pie ingredients
- $\frac{3}{8}$ kg butter
- $\frac{1}{4}$ kg flour
- $\frac{1}{10}$ kg sugar
- $\frac{4}{5}$ kg apples

Challenge 2

1. These ingredients are for 1 pizza. The chef wants to cook 6 pizzas. Work out how much of each ingredient he needs.

Pizza ingredients
- $\frac{3}{10}$ kg flour
- $\frac{2}{6}$ litre of water
- $\frac{3}{8}$ litre of tomato sauce
- $\frac{2}{5}$ kg mozzarella cheese
- $\frac{2}{3}$ kg mushrooms

2 These ingredients are for 2 cakes.
   The chef wants to cook 8 cakes.
   Work out how much of each ingredient
   he needs. Write your answers as
   mixed numbers.

   Cake ingredients
   $\frac{4}{10}$ kg sugar
   $\frac{2}{7}$ kg butter
   $\frac{3}{8}$ kg flour
   $\frac{2}{20}$ kg cocoa powder
   $\frac{1}{4}$ teaspoon baking powder
   $\frac{3}{5}$ kg icing sugar

3 These pizzas are shared out between five friends.
   How much of a whole pizza will each person get?

   a $\frac{3}{4}$ b $\frac{2}{3}$ c $\frac{4}{5}$ d $\frac{3}{5}$ e $\frac{5}{8}$

Challenge 3

1 Choose three fractions from below and add them
   together. Work out the answer to each fraction
   calculation, writing your answer in its simplest form.
   Make six different fraction calculations in this way.

   $\frac{1}{2}$ $\frac{1}{8}$ $\frac{1}{4}$ $\frac{3}{4}$ $\frac{7}{8}$

   $\frac{2}{5}$ $\frac{3}{8}$ $\frac{5}{6}$ $\frac{3}{5}$ $\frac{1}{6}$

2 Choose 3 fractions from above. Add two of the fractions
   together and subtract the third. Work out the answer to each
   fraction calculation, writing your answer in its simplest form.
   Make six different fraction calculations in this way.

Unit 7, Week 2, Lesson 1

Proportion problems

Recognise and solve proportion problems

Challenge 1

A factory produces mixed boxes of flavoured crisps. The different flavours are always produced in the same proportions. For every 2 salt and vinegar packets, there are 4 packets of plain crisps, 3 packets of cheese and onion crisps and 1 packet of prawn cocktail crisps.

a How many packets of salt and vinegar flavour are there if the total number of packets is:

  i 50?   ii 120?   iii 700?   iv 5000?

b What is the total number of packets of crisps if there are:

  i 12 packets of prawn cocktail?

  ii 12 packets of plain?

  iii 12 packets of cheese and onion?

  iv 12 packets of salt and vinegar?

Challenge 2

1 A pizza factory produces 4 different types of pizza. The different flavours are always produced in the same proportions. For every 4 cheese pizzas, there are 5 pepperoni pizzas, 2 mushroom pizzas and 1 chicken pizza.

a How many cheese pizzas are there if the total number of pizzas is:

  i 48?   ii 120?   iii 600?   iv 3600?

b What is the total number of pizzas if there are:

  i 150 cheese pizzas?   ii 150 pepperoni pizzas?

  iii 150 mushroom pizzas?   iv 150 chicken pizzas?

2 A warehouse has boxes of beanie hats.

   a The proportion of blue beanie hats in a box is 3 out of 20. Suggest four sets of numbers of blue and other colour hats that could be in the box.

   b For each of the total numbers of hats you calculated in a, choose a different colour and a different proportion out of 20 and calculate the numbers based on your new colour.

3 The proportion of red cars in the car park is always the same at 2 out of 15.

   a How many red cars are there when there are:

      i 30 cars?   ii 90 cars?   iii 195 cars?

   b How many cars are parked when the number of red cars is:

      i 10?   ii 22?   iii 32?

   c When the car park is full, there are 40 red cars. What is the capacity of the car park?

Challenge 3

1 A sweet factory produces 5 different chocolate bars. The different flavours are always produced in the same proportions. For every 3 coconut flavoured bars, there are 5 honeycomb, 1 coffee, 7 orange and 4 strawberry.

   a How many coconut flavoured bars are there if the total number of chocolate bars is:

      i 40?   ii 200?   iii 960?   iv 4800?

   b What is the total number of chocolate bars if there are:

      i 100 strawberry flavoured bars?
      ii 280 orange flavoured bars?
      iii 79 coffee flavoured bars?
      iv 255 honeycomb flavoured bars?

2 In a town with a population of 7680 adults, 1 driver in every 9 has an advanced driver qualification. 3 out of every 4 adults in the city are drivers.
   How many advanced drivers are there in the town?

Unit 7, Week 2, Lesson 2

Ratio and scale factors

- Use ratios to solve problems
- Solve scale factor problems

Challenge 1

1 Write each ratio in its simplest form.

a 6 : 12   b 6 : 18   c 24 : 30   d 28 : 21

e 45 : 81   f 42 : 60   g 50 : 60   h 55 : 121

2 Look at the bead necklaces below.

a In each case, write the ratio of triangular to circular beads.

b What is the proportion of triangular beads in each necklace?

3 These two triangles are similar.

a Find the scale factor.

b Calculate the missing lengths of the larger triangle.

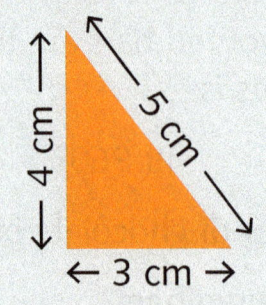

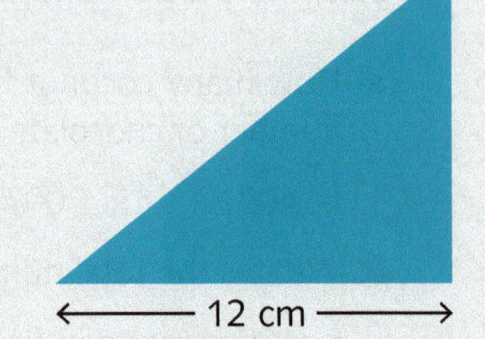

Challenge 2

1 Look at the bead necklaces below.

a In each case, write the ratio of triangular : circular : square beads.

b What is the proportion of triangular beads in each necklace?

2 Here are three similar scalene triangles. Find the scale factor for each triangle and calculate the missing lengths.

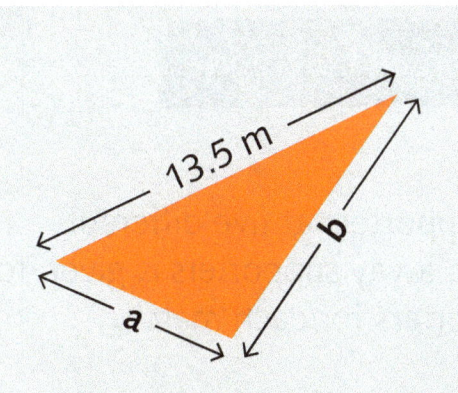

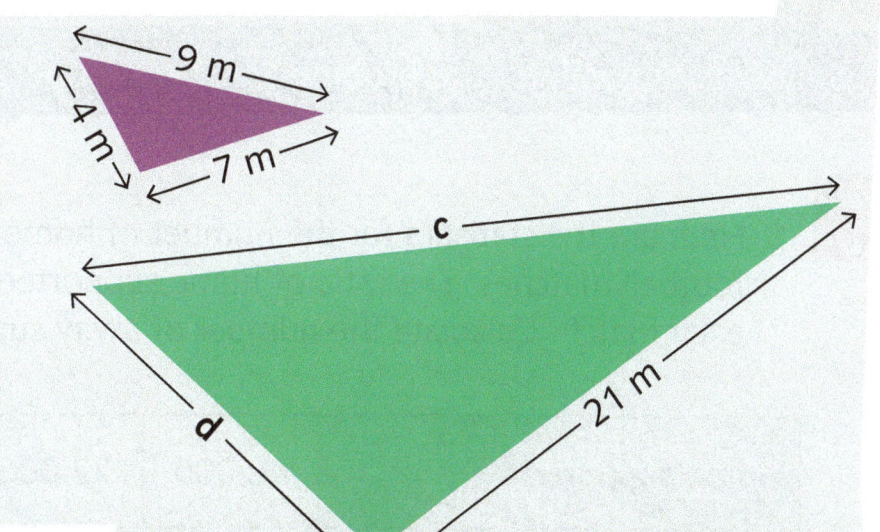

3 The numbers of children in a junior school have been recorded here.

a Use the information in the table to calculate:

　i the number of boys and girls in each year group

　ii the number of boys in the school

　iii the number of girls in the school.

b One new boy joins the school. What is the ratio of boys to girls in the whole school now?

Year group	Total number of children	Ratio of boys to girls
Y3	80	5 : 3
Y4	84	3 : 4
Y5	90	8 : 7
Y6	85	9 : 8

Challenge 3

You have red and blue beads.

a Determine at least five different patterns of beads that can be used to make a necklace of exactly 30 beads with a repeating pattern. Calculate the ratios of beads in the simplest form.

b Can you list all the possible repeating patterns?

Unit 7, Week 2, Lesson 3

Ratio problems

Solve missing value ratio problems using multiplication and division

Challenge 1

1. Here are the statistics for the number of home supporters at five different football matches. The ratio of home supporters to away supporters is given for each match. Calculate the number of away supporters for each match.

Home supporters	48 000	72 000	55 000	63 000	39 000
Ratio of home : away supporters	8 : 1	6 : 1	10 : 1	9 : 2	13 : 2

2. Look at each pair of statements and decide if the second statement is true or false and explain why, or give the correct answer for any that are false.

   a. Grey paint is 1 part black paint to 4 parts white paint. In a 10 *l* tin of grey paint, there are 8 *l* of white paint.

   b. The ratio of boys to girls in a class is 3 : 2. In a class of 30 children, there are 12 girls.

   c. Sam spent €100 on clothes and CDs in the ratio 3 : 2. He spent €40 on clothes.

Challenge 2

1. Here are two strawberry smoothie recipes.

   Strawberry and nectarine smoothie
   Serves 4
   - 12 strawberries
   - 3 nectarines
   - 4 apples

   Strawberry and banana smoothie
   Serves 3
   - 16 strawberries
   - 1 banana
   - 1 orange
   - 4 apples

   a. Calculate the amount of each ingredient required for each recipe to serve 12.

   b. Which smoothie has a higher ratio of strawberry to apple?

   c. How many people can you serve one smoothie to if you have 24 oranges and 24 nectarines but unlimited quantities of the other fruits?

2 Here is a recipe for Chocolate Fudge Brownies.

> **Chocolate Fudge Brownie**
> **Serves 12**
> • 180 g chocolate
> • 120 g butter
> • 200 g brown sugar
> • 6 ml vanilla extract
> • 2 eggs
> • 180 g plain flour
> • 100 g chocolate chips

a Write the following ratios in their simplest form:
  i chocolate : butter
  ii chocolate : brown sugar
  iii chocolate : chocolate chips
  iv brown sugar : chocolate chips

b How many servings are there if you use:
  i 15 ml vanilla extract?
  ii a dozen eggs?
  iii 1 kg brown sugar?
  iv 60 g butter?

3 Look at each pair of statements and decide if the second statement is true or false. Explain why, or give the correct answer for any that are false.

a Grey paint is 1 part black paint to 4 parts white paint. In a 2 *l* tin of paint, there is 1·6 *l* of white paint.

b The ratio of boys to girls in a class is 4 : 5. In a class of 27 children, there are 15 girls.

c 200 kg of sand is divided into piles in the ratio 2 : 3. The smaller pile is 80 kg.

d The approximate ratio of time asleep : time awake for a newborn baby is 2 : 1. A baby is awake for 56 hours in a week.

Challenge 3

Look at each pair of statements and decide if the second statement is true or false.

a Purple paint is 4 parts blue paint to 3 parts red paint. In a 3·5 *l* tin of paint, there is 1·5 *l* of red paint.

b The ratio of boys to girls in a class is 7 : 8. In a class of 30 children, there are 16 girls.

c Three Year 6 classes collected money for charity. The money they raised was in the ratio 7 : 6 : 5. Two of the classes raised €126 and €110.

d 260 kg of sand is divided into piles in the ratio 6 : 7. The smaller pile is 120 kg.

Unit 7, Week 2, Lesson 4

Ratio and proportion problems

Solve problems involving unequal sharing and grouping using knowledge of fractions and multiples

Cauliflower Cheese for 4

- 1 cauliflower (about 700 g)
- 40 g butter
- 40 g plain flour
- 450 ml milk
- 100 g grated cheddar cheese
- 20 g breadcrumbs (optional)

Challenge 1

1. This cauliflower cheese recipe serves 4.

   a Write the cauliflower cheese recipe for 6 people.

   b Explain your method.

   c Discuss your method with a partner and see if you did it in the same way

2. Orange squash concentrate is mixed with water in the ratio 1 : 6 to make drinks. How much squash can be made from:

   a 200 ml of concentrate?   b 4 l of concentrate?

Challenge 2

1. A pancake recipe says that for every egg you need 3 spoonfuls of plain flour and 2 cups of milk. This is enough mixture to make 4 small pancakes.

   a Write the ingredients required for 4 eggs. How many pancakes will this make?

   b You want to make 100 pancakes for a party. Calculate the amount of ingredients required.

2. A paint company mixes paint in the following ratios:

   Puzzling purple – 4 red : 5 blue : 1 white

   Outrageous orange – 3 red : 6 yellow : 1 white

   Pretty pink – 6 red : 9 white

   Groovy grey – 3 black : 5 white

   Bold brown – 4 red : 3 blue : 1 yellow

66

a How many litres of each paint do you need to make 20 litres of each colour?

b Stocks of red paint are very low, with only 12 *l* left.

  i What colour should the company make to give the largest quantity?

  ii Calculate how many litres can be made.

3 A restaurant buys a box of mixed red, green and yellow peppers.

- There is a minimum of 100 peppers in every box.
- There is a maximum of 115 peppers in every box.
- The proportion of red peppers in the box is 2 out of 5.
- The ratio of yellow to green peppers is 1 : 2.

What are the possible numbers of each colour of pepper?

Challenge 3

Three animal charities raised money for pandas, tigers and elephants at an outdoor event in a field. The field was shared in the ratio 2 : 3 : 5 according to the amount of money each charity paid to take part. At the event, the charities then raised a total of €3000.

a How much would each charity have raised if the money they collected was in the same ratio as the area of the field they were using?

b The actual amount collected by each charity was €1000 for pandas, €800 for tigers and €1200 for elephants. Express this ratio in its simplest form.

c The tiger charity paid €150 for its space in the field. Calculate which charity made the most profit overall.

Unit 7, Week 3, Lesson 1

Water sports centre pie charts

Interpret and draw pie charts and use them to solve problems

These pie charts show the children's favourite activities at the water sports centre over four weeks. Each sector in these pie charts represents 10%.

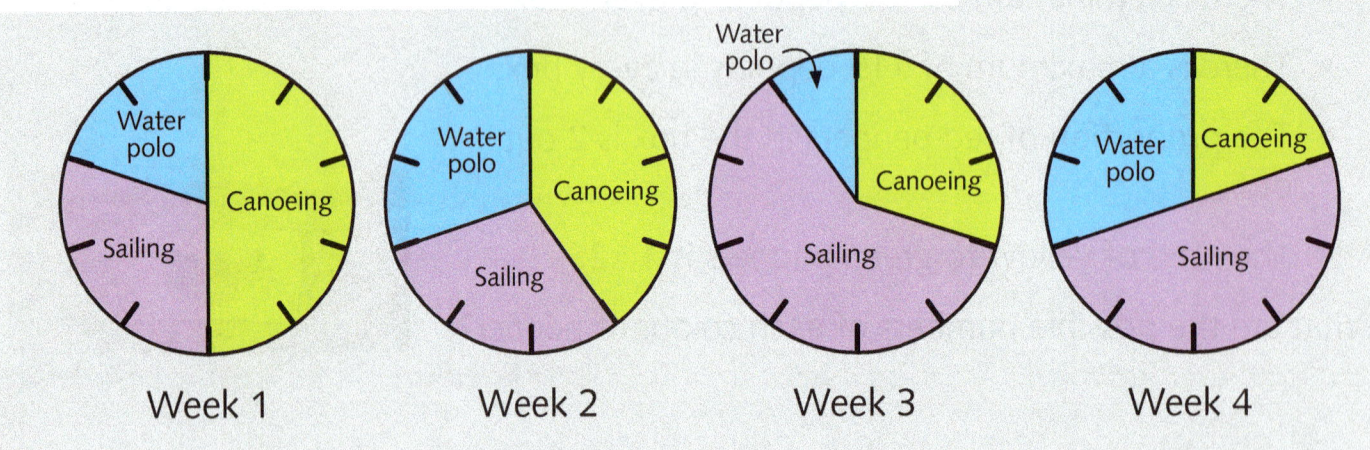

Week 1   Week 2   Week 3   Week 4

Challenge 1

Copy the table below. Then use the data in the pie charts above to find the percentage of children who chose each activity as their favourite.

Activity	Week 1	Week 2	Week 3	Week 4
Canoeing	50%			
Sailing				
Water polo				

Challenges 2, 3

1 Use the information in the pie charts at the top of the page to complete the database in Resource 48: Database.

You will need:
- Resource 48: Database
- ruler
- four coloured pencils

68

2 Use your database to find out in which week:

   a equal numbers of children chose sailing and water polo

   b twice as many children chose sailing than canoeing

   c more children chose water polo than canoeing

   d 8 more children chose canoeing than sailing

   e 6 fewer children chose canoeing than water polo.

3 Which two weeks had the same number of children who preferred:

   a canoeing?   b sailing?

4 Complete the pie charts on Resource 48: Database to show the information below for Weeks 5 and 6. Colour each pie chart and complete its key.

Week	Total number of children	Number of children choosing each activity			
		Canoeing	Sailing	Water polo	Rafting
5	60	24	18	12	6
6	60	15	24	9	12

Challenge 3

Look at your completed pie charts on Resource 48.

1 Write three statements that describe how the pie charts for Weeks 5 and 6 are similar or different from each other.

2 Write three questions about the pie charts for Weeks 5 and 6 for a partner to answer.

69

Unit 7, Week 3, Lesson 2

Using line graphs

Construct and use line graphs to solve problems

Challenge 1

1. Copy the table below. Then use the relationship 8 km ≈ 5 miles to complete it.

Kilometres	0	8	16	24	32	80
Miles	0	5				

You will need:
- 1 cm squared paper
- ruler

2. Use the data from the completed table in Question 1 to draw a line graph for converting between miles and kilometres. Make sure you join the points with a straight line and that your graph is big enough to extend your line to the point (80, 50).

3. Use your graph to convert these distances to kilometres.

   a 25 miles   b 30 miles   c 45 miles

4. Use your graph to convert these distances to miles.

   a 20 km   b 28 km   c 44 km

Challenge 2

1. Copy the table below. Then use the relationship 6 minutes to travel a distance of 5 kilometres to complete it.

Time (min)	0	6	12	18	24	72
Distance (km)	0	5				

You will need:
- 1 cm squared paper
- ruler

2. Use the data from the completed table in Question 1 to draw a time distance graph. Make sure you join the points with a straight line and that your graph is big enough to extend your line to the point (72, 60).

3. Find the distance travelled in: a 36 minutes   b 60 minutes

4. Find the time taken to travel: a 35 km   b 45 km

5 The graph on the right shows that a taxi driver charges €2 for a pick-up fee and €1.50 per kilometre.

Journey cost

a What is the cost for a journey of:

   i   2 kilometres?
   ii 6 kilometre?
   iii 10 kilometres?
   iv 5 kilometres?

b What distance was travelled if the fare was:

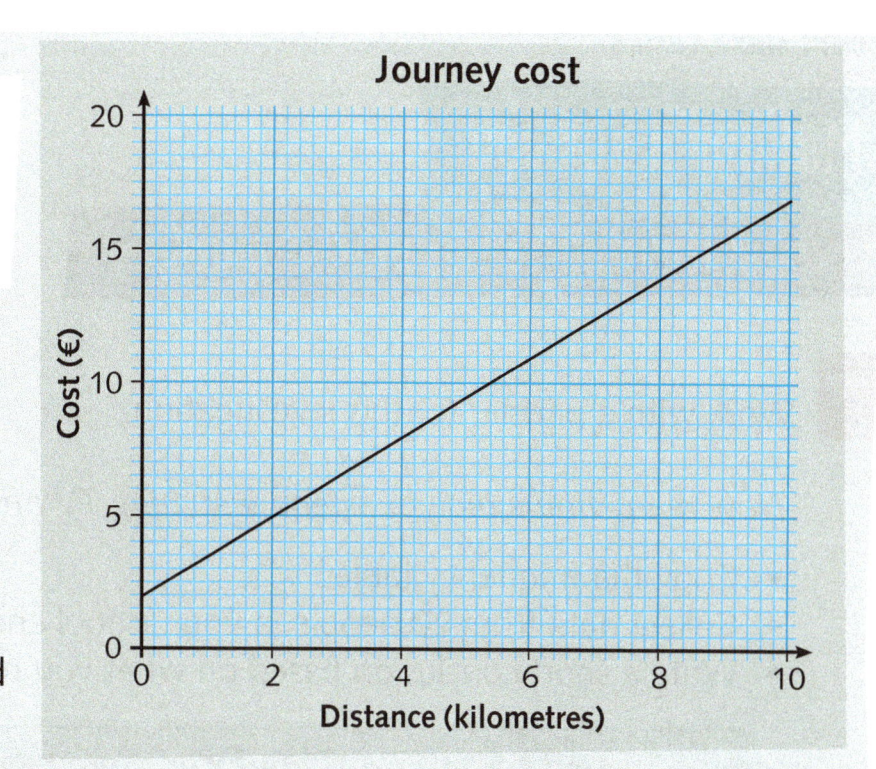

   i €12.50?   ii €15.50?

Challenge 3

A function machine converts °F to °C using the rule:

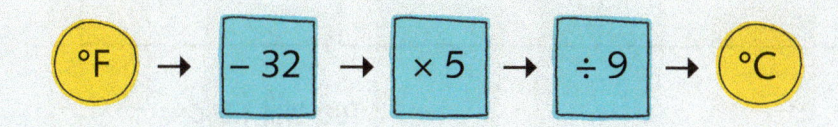

°F → − 32 → × 5 → ÷ 9 → °C

You will need:
- Resource 49: °F to °C graph paper
- 1 cm squared paper
- ruler

1 Copy the table below. Use the function machine to complete the values for °C rounded to the nearest degree.

°F	32	41	61	82	95	110
°C						

City	°F	°C
Boston	77	
Canberra	52	
Madrid	81	
Tokyo	72	
Dubai	102	
Luxor	106	
Paris	66	
Bangkok	91	

2 Plot the points on Resource 49: °F to °C graph paper and draw the conversion graph.

3 Copy the table on the right and use your graph to convert the temperatures to °C, to the nearest degree.

71

Unit 7, Week 3, Lesson 3

Making a survey

Collect and organise data to solve problems

Challenge 1

Work with a partner for this investigation.

How many hours did you spend watching TV after school yesterday?

- Copy the frequency table.
- Collect data from 20 people in your school and complete your frequency table.
- Write a short conclusion based on what you have found out.

Time spent watching TV	Tally	Frequency
None		
Up to 1 hour		
More than 1 hour but less than 2 hours		
2 hours or more		

Challenge 2

Work with a partner. Choose one of the following investigations to answer: Question 1 or Question 2.

You will need:
- 1 cm squared paper
- ruler

1 *How many hours did you spend playing computer games after school yesterday?*

- Copy the frequency table.
- Collect data from 20 people in your school and complete your frequency table.
- Illustrate your report with suitable diagrams or graphs and explain why you have used them.
- Write a short conclusion based on what you have found out.

Time spent playing computer games	Tally	Frequency
None		
Up to 1 hour		
More than 1 hour but less than 2 hours		
2 hours or more		

2 *Which of these activities do you do outside school?*

- Copy the frequency table.
- Collect data from 20 people in your school and complete your frequency table.
- Illustrate your report with suitable diagrams or graphs and explain why you have used them.
- Write a short conclusion based on what you have found out.

Activity	Tally	Frequency
Football		
Swimming		
Dance		
Something else		
No outside school activity		

Challenge 3

Work with a partner. Survey 20 or more people in your school and ask them two questions:

A *How much pocket money do you get per week?*

B *What do you spend most of your pocket money on?*

- Design your own frequency table for **A**. Give a choice of four responses, for example: 'None','Less than €2', '€2 to €5', or 'More than €5'.
- Devise a questionnaire for **B**. Give a choice of four responses, for example: 'Sweets', 'Sport', 'Music' or 'Other'.
- Illustrate your report with suitable diagrams or graphs and explain why you have used them.
- Write a short conclusion based on what you have found out.

You will need:

- 1 cm squared paper
- ruler

Unit 7, Week 3, Lesson 4

Finding the mean

Calculate and interpret the mean as an average of a set of data

Example

5 + 9 + 4 = 18

18 ÷ 3 = 6

Mean = 6

Challenge 1

Find the mean value of each set of cards.

a 8, 6, 7

b 7, 2, 9

c 10, 4, 9, 9

d 5, 6, 6, 3

Challenge 2

1 Find the mean of each set of numbers.

   a 4   8   12   16
   b 3   9   15   21
   c 5   15   25   35
   d 9   11   17   23

2 Four trays of sandwiches have been prepared for lunch.

   a How many sandwiches are on each tray?
   b Calculate the mean number of sandwiches per tray.

   A    B    C 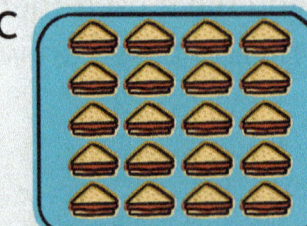   D

74

3 The table below shows the number of goals scored in six games by players in the school's netball team.

   a Find the mean number of goals scored by each player.

   b Find the mean number of goals scored per game.

Player	Number of goals					
	Game 1	Game 2	Game 3	Game 4	Game 5	Game 6
Donna	2	1	2	3	3	1
Leah	4	3	5	1	3	2
Maria	3	5	4	2	0	4
Tanya	3	6	1	3	3	5

4 The table shows the distance run by each athlete in five training sessions. Calculate the mean distance run by each athlete in one training session.

Athlete	Distance (km)
Marek	45
Jonny	32·5
Jordan	37
Simon	41·5

Challenge 3

The height of a pony is measured in hands. The table shows the height in hands of Jack, Jenny, Julie and Jingle. The mean height of the five ponies is 13 hands. What height is Joyce in hands?

Pony	Hands
Jack	15
Jenny	11
Julie	12
Jingle	13
Joyce	

75

Unit 8, Week 1, Lesson 1

Division HTO ÷ TO using the expanded written method

- Use the expanded written method of long division to calculate HTO ÷ TO
- Estimate and check the answer to a calculation

Challenge 1

Work out the answer to each calculation.

1. a 26 × 3
   b 26 × 30
2. a 37 × 8
   b 37 × 80
3. a 19 × 6
   b 19 × 60
4. a 45 × 7
   b 45 × 70
5. a 84 × 9
   b 84 × 90

6. a 63 × 4
   b 63 × 40
7. a 90 × 7
   b 90 × 70
8. a 28 × 5
   b 28 × 50
9. a 33 × 6
   b 33 × 60
10. a 9 × 54
    b 90 × 54

11. a 7 × 42
    b 70 × 42
12. a 58 × 6
    b 60 × 58
13. a 8 × 81
    b 81 × 80
14. a 5 × 11
    b 50 × 11
15. a 71 × 4
    b 40 × 71

Challenge 2

1. For each division calculation write your estimate, then use the expanded written method to work out the answer. Record any remainders as a fraction. Be sure to compare your answer with your estimate.

Example

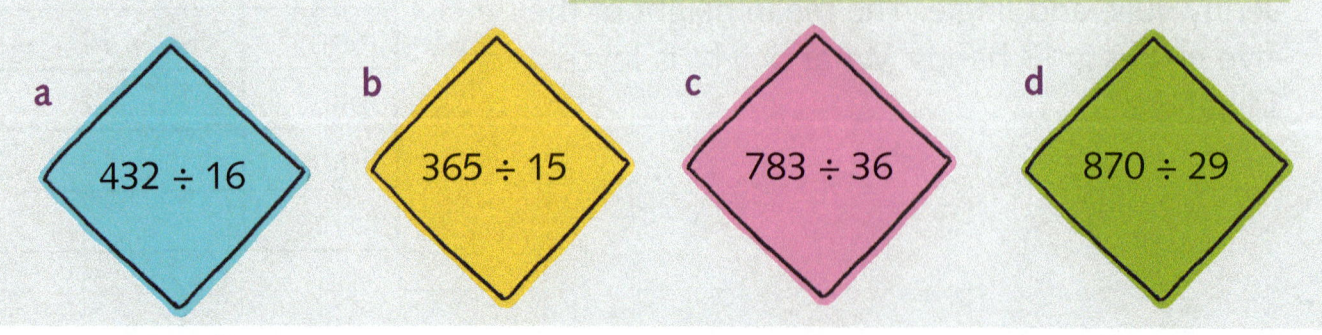

644 ÷ 14 → 600 ÷ 10 = 60 or 600 ÷ 15 = 40

```
        H T O
          4 6
      ┌─────────
   14 │ 6 4 4
      −  5 6 0    (40 × 14)
      ─────────
          8 4
      −   8 4    (6 × 14)
      ─────────
            0
```

a 432 ÷ 16

b 365 ÷ 15

c 783 ÷ 36

d 870 ÷ 29

- e 686 ÷ 23
- f 770 ÷ 22
- g 596 ÷ 14
- h 775 ÷ 25
- i 836 ÷ 19
- j 756 ÷ 14

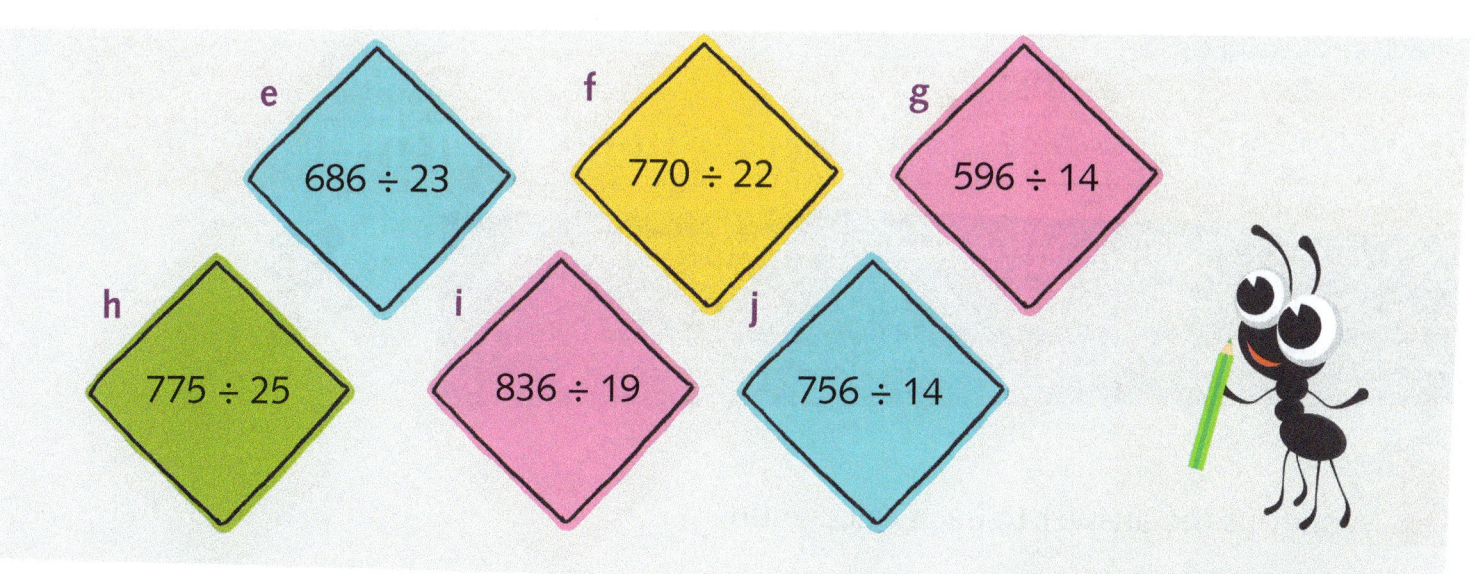

2 Play this game with a partner.
- Choose one number from each box.
- Divide the 3-digit number by the 2-digit number, and write the answer as a whole number.
- Your score is the remainder.
- Your partner checks your working, then takes a turn to choose a different pair of numbers.
- After 4 rounds, add together all your remainders. The winner is the player with the largest total.

924	561	349	294
373	835	573	602
256	787	136	728
162	448	615	819

26	54	45	97
62	89	73	38
17	43	84	99
64	51	32	76

Challenge 3

1 Find the answer to each of these problems.

a If a plane travels at 506 kilometres per hour, how far would it travel in 1 minute?

b A plane travels at 840 km per hour. If it is 196 km east of its destination, how long will it take to reach the destination?

c A car uses 882 litres of petrol in a fortnight. How many litres does it use on average per day?

d The total bill for 24 nights hotel accommodation is €936. How much does it cost per night?

2 Write down five situations when you would need to divide to find the answer.

Unit 8, Week 1, Lesson 2

Division ThHTO ÷ TO using the expanded written method

- Use the expanded written method of long division to calculate ThHTO ÷ TO
- Estimate and check the answer to a calculation

Challenge 1

Work out the answer to each calculation.

1. a 24 × 100
   b 42 × 100
2. a 67 × 100
   b 76 × 100
3. a 59 × 100
   b 95 × 100
4. a 36 × 7
   b 36 × 700

5. a 57 × 4
   b 57 × 400
6. a 49 × 9
   b 49 × 900
7. a 85 × 5
   b 85 × 500
8. a 64 × 2
   b 64 × 200

Challenge 2

1. For each division calculation write your estimate, then use the expanded written method to work out the answer. Record any remainders as a fraction. Be sure to compare your answer with your estimate.

Example

5832 ÷ 18 → 6000 ÷ 20 = 300 or 5400 ÷ 18 = 300

```
     Th H T O
          3 2 4
   18 5 8 3 2
    -  5 4 0 0   (300 × 18)
         ³4 ¹³3 2
    -      3 6 0  (20 × 18)
             7 2
    -        7 2  (4 × 18)
               0
```

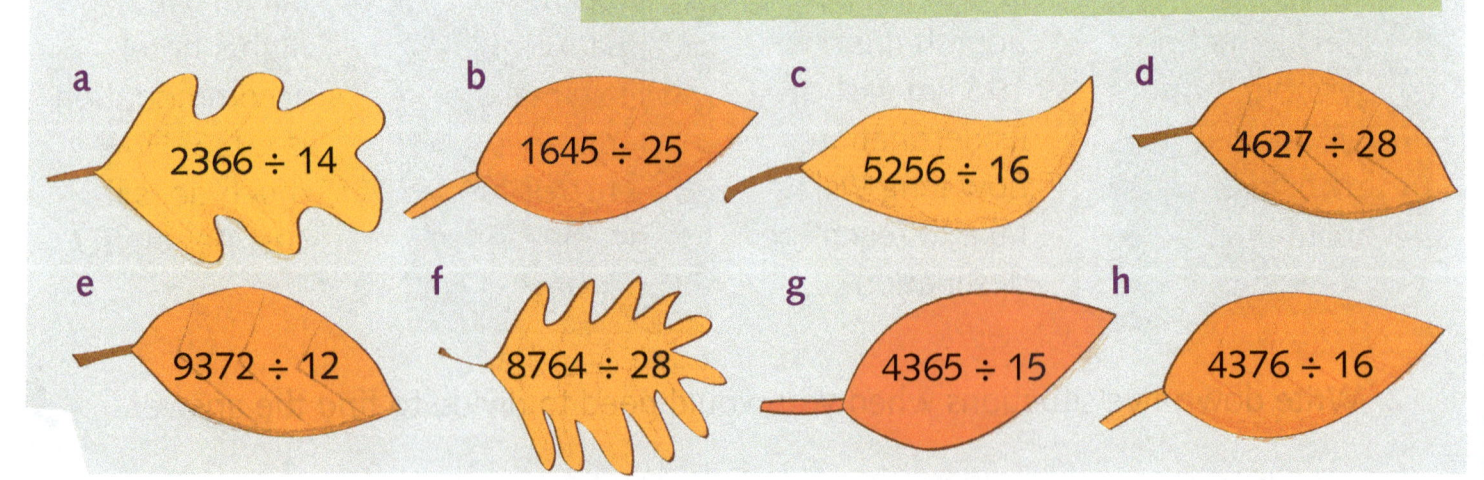

a 2366 ÷ 14
b 1645 ÷ 25
c 5256 ÷ 16
d 4627 ÷ 28
e 9372 ÷ 12
f 8764 ÷ 28
g 4365 ÷ 15
h 4376 ÷ 16

2   Play this game with a partner.

   - Choose one number from each box.
   - Divide the 4-digit number by the 2-digit number, and write the answer as a whole number.
   - Your score is the remainder.
   - Your partner checks your working, then takes a turn to choose a different pair of numbers.
   - After 4 rounds, add together all your remainders. The winner is the player with the largest total.

2073	4296	1314	7632
3424	5189	6505	8757
9148	7260	3873	2618
5495	6387	1901	4526

75	31	56	81
26	47	18	67
62	92	35	43
34	53	14	29

Challenge 3

The answer to five of these calculations is 49. Can you find which ones?

1225 ÷ 25

1127 ÷ 23

1104 ÷ 24

882 ÷ 18

588 ÷ 12

1296 ÷ 27

1764 ÷ 36

1034 ÷ 22

1472 ÷ 32

79

Unit 8, Week 1, Lesson 3

Division HTO ÷ TO using the formal written method

- Use the formal written method of long division to calculate HTO ÷ TO
- Estimate and check the answer to a calculation

Challenge 1

Work out the answers to these mentally.

1 a 150 ÷ 15
   b 360 ÷ 36
   c 620 ÷ 62
   d 240 ÷ 24
   e 310 ÷ 31

2 a 240 ÷ 12
   b 480 ÷ 24
   c 450 ÷ 15
   d 360 ÷ 18
   e 390 ÷ 13

3 a 550 ÷ 11
   b 600 ÷ 12
   c 560 ÷ 14
   d 840 ÷ 12
   e 340 ÷ 17

4 a 640 ÷ 20
   b 390 ÷ 30
   c 450 ÷ 50
   d 810 ÷ 90
   e 540 ÷ 60

Challenge 2

1 For each division calculation write your estimate, then use the formal written method to work out the answer. Record any remainders as a fraction in its simplest form. Be sure to compare your answer with your estimate.

Example

644 ÷ 14 → 600 ÷ 10 = 60 or 600 ÷ 15 = 40

```
         4 6
    14 ) 6 4 4
       - 5 6 ↓
           8 4
         - 8 4
             0
```

a 398 ÷ 24
b 645 ÷ 15
c 526 ÷ 16
d 632 ÷ 28
e 961 ÷ 17
f 676 ÷ 24
g 846 ÷ 14
h 245 ÷ 13
i 488 ÷ 24
j 475 ÷ 25
k 780 ÷ 25
l 1596 ÷ 18

2 Copy and complete these division calculations, writing in the missing digits.

a)
```
        2 □ r □
27 ) 6 0 2
   - □ 4 ↓
       6 □
     - □ 4
       ___
         □
```

b)
```
        □ 3 r □
18 ) 7 8 1
   - □ 2 ↓
       □ 1
     - □ □
       ___
         □
```

c)
```
        2 □ r □ □
37 ) 8 7 3
   - 7 □ ↓
       1 □ 3
     - □ 1 1
       ___
         □ □
```

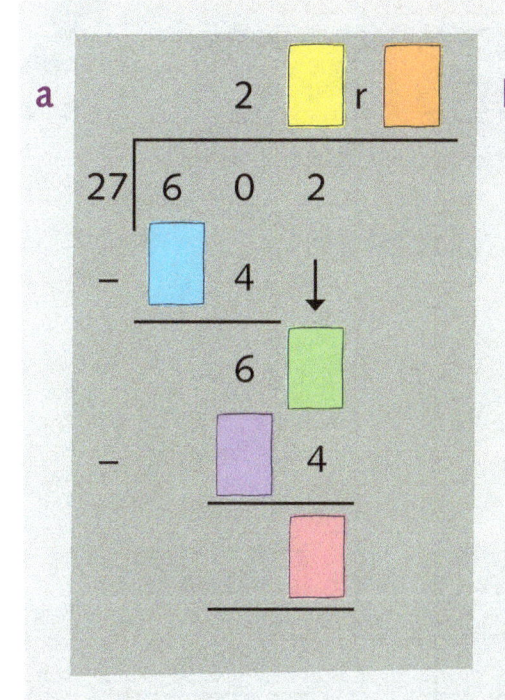

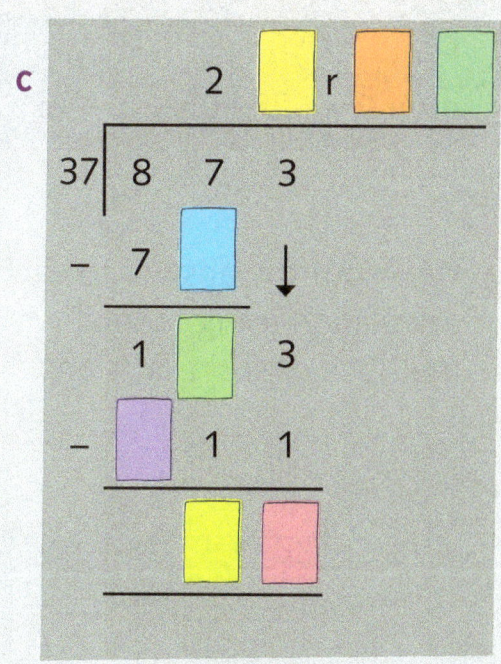

Challenge 3

Find the answer to each of these problems.

a There are 792 books. The same number of books is placed onto 18 different shelves. How many books are placed onto each shelf?

b A carton contains 672 pencils altogether. The pencils are in boxes of 12. How many boxes of pencils are there in the carton?

c 770 packed lunches are shared equally between 35 classes. How many children in each class receive a packed lunch?

d 912 playground items are shared equally among 24 classes. How many items does each class receive?

Unit 8, Week 1, Lesson 4

Division ThHTO ÷ TO using the formal written method

- Use the formal written method of long division to calculate ThHTO ÷ TO
- Estimate and check the answer to a calculation

Challenge 1

Work out the answer to each calculation using mental methods or short division.

Example

$245 ÷ 4$

$245 ÷ 4 = (240 + 5) ÷ 4$
$= 60 + 1 \text{ r } 1$
$= 61 \text{ r } 1$

$4 \overline{)245} = 61 \text{ r } 1$

a	÷ 4
i	329
ii	154
iii	284
iv	447
v	208

b	÷ 8
i	357
ii	435
iii	256
iv	188
v	571

c	÷ 6
i	378
ii	488
iii	256
iv	639
v	565

d	÷ 9
i	279
ii	549
iii	631
iv	452
v	723

Challenge 2

For each division calculation write your estimate, then use the formal written method to work out the answer.
Record any remainders as a fraction in its simplest form. Be sure to compare your answer with your estimate.

Example

$5832 ÷ 18 \rightarrow 6000 ÷ 20 = 300$
or $5400 ÷ 18 = 300$

$18 \overline{)5832} = 324$

a $8436 ÷ 12$
b $9875 ÷ 25$
c $9352 ÷ 21$
d $6464 ÷ 18$
e $7370 ÷ 15$
f $5391 ÷ 18$
g $8866 ÷ 26$
h $3080 ÷ 35$

Challenge 3

1. Deepa is training for the marathon. Calculate how far she jogs per day over the periods of time shown below. Copy and complete the table. Show your working.

Period of time	1 day	1 week	1 fortnight	Month of May	6-week summer holidays
Total distance run (km)	14	182	392	1178	2016
Distance run per day (km)					

2. Rearrange each set of 6 digits in the vertices of the hexagon to make a ThHTO ÷ TO division calculation that equals the number in the circle.

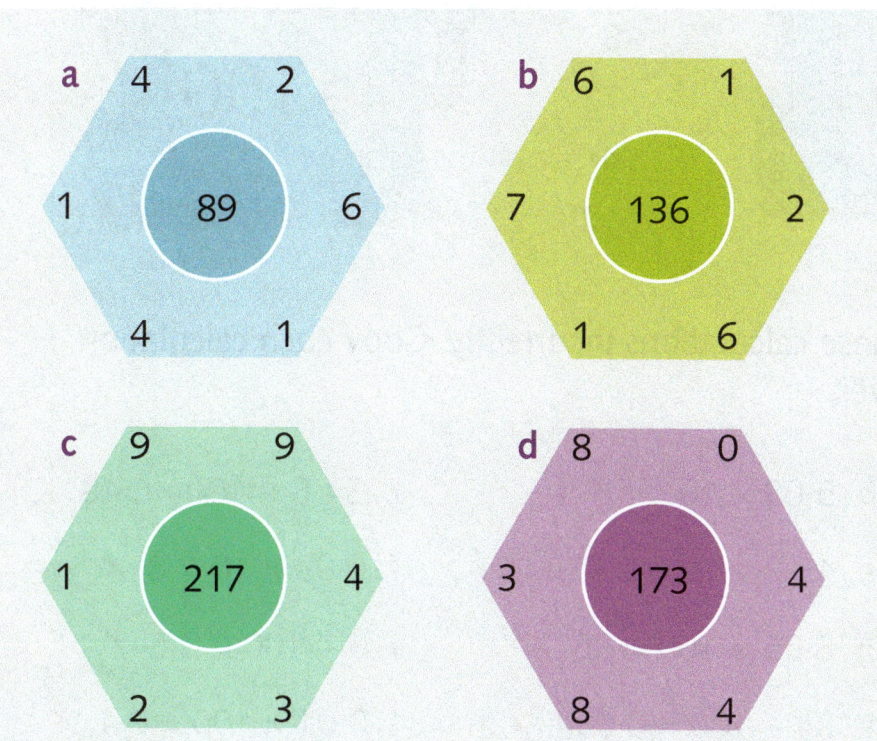

a) 4   2
   1 [89] 6
    4   1

b) 6   1
   7 [136] 2
    1   6

c) 9   9
   1 [217] 4
    2   3

d) 8   0
   3 [173] 4
    8   4

Hint
- The four digits at the top of the hexagon are the digits that make up the 4-digit number.
- The two digits at the bottom of the hexagon are the digits that make up the 2-digit number.

Unit 8, Week 2, Lesson 1

Dividing decimals using mental methods and the formal written method

- Use mental methods to divide a decimal by a 1-digit number
- Use the formal written method of short division to divide a decimal by a 1-digit number

Challenge 1

1 For each machine, work out the output number for each input number.

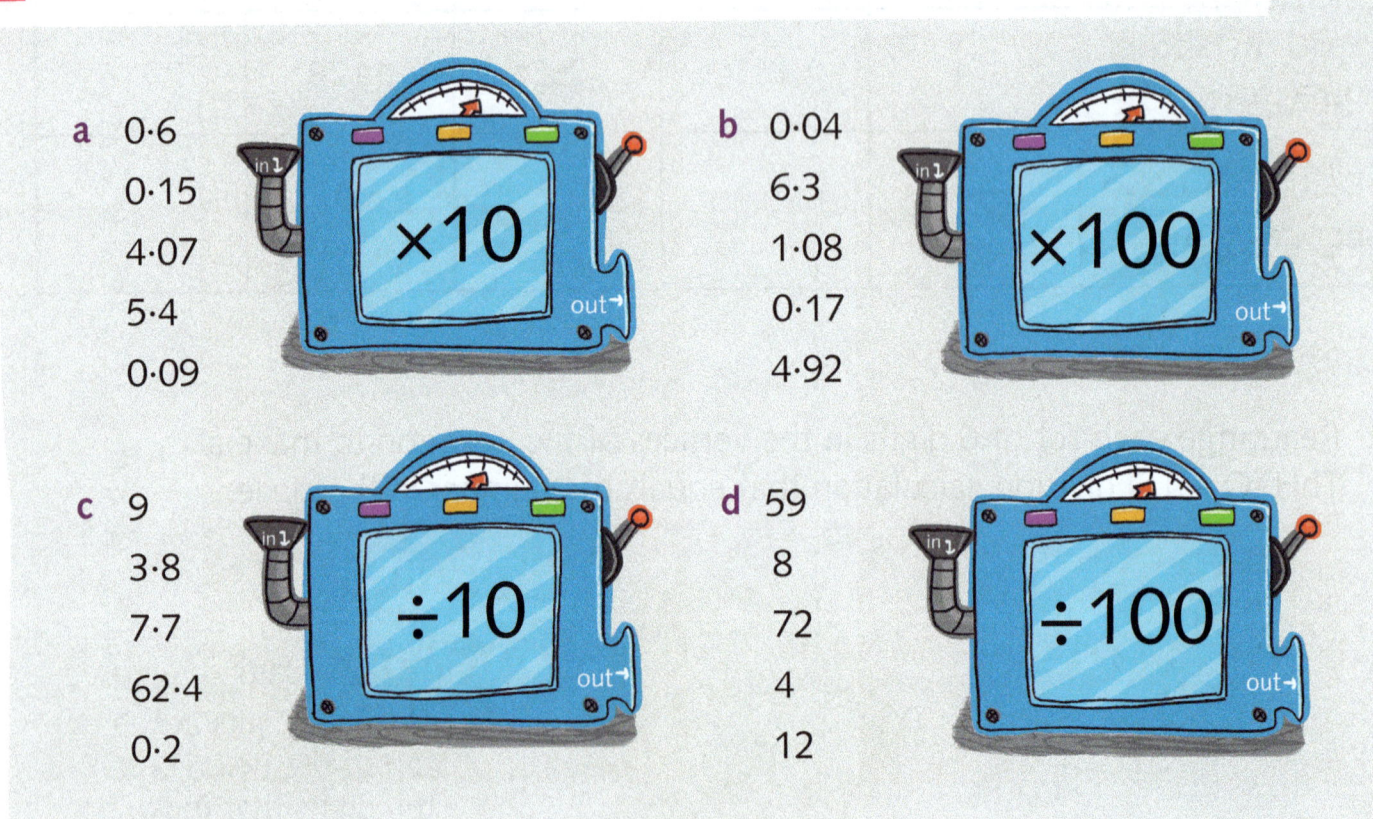

a ×10
- 0·6
- 0·15
- 4·07
- 5·4
- 0·09

b ×100
- 0·04
- 6·3
- 1·08
- 0·17
- 4·92

c ÷10
- 9
- 3·8
- 7·7
- 62·4
- 0·2

d ÷100
- 59
- 8
- 72
- 4
- 12

2 Malik answered each of these calculations incorrectly. Copy each calculation and write the correct answer.

a 0·3 × 10 = 30 ✗
b 5·08 × 10 = 58 ✗
c 34·8 × 100 = 348 ✗
d 18 ÷ 100 = 1·8 ✗
e 43·7 ÷ 10 = 0·437 ✗
f 0·08 × 10 = 8 ✗
g 4·1 ÷ 10 = 41 ✗
h 8·05 × 100 = 85 ✗
i 6 ÷ 100 = 0·6 ✗
j 13 ÷ 10 = 0·13 ✗
k 34 ÷ 100 = 0·034 ✗
l 0·01 × 100 = 0·1 ✗

Challenge 2

1. Sort the calculations into two groups: those you can work out using mental methods and those where you need to use a written method.

- 93·6 ÷ 3
- 73·6 ÷ 4
- 7·52 ÷ 8
- 54·4 ÷ 8
- 5·22 ÷ 9
- 69·6 ÷ 3
- 8·19 ÷ 9
- 68·5 ÷ 5
- 35·7 ÷ 7
- 46·4 ÷ 8
- 4·68 ÷ 9
- 7·49 ÷ 7
- 16·8 ÷ 4
- 6·27 ÷ 3

2. Work out the answer to each calculation in Question 1. For the calculations that need a written method, use the formal written method of short division. Remember to estimate the answer first.

Example

27·6 ÷ 6 → 30 ÷ 6 = 5

```
    T O · t h
        4 · 6
  6 ) 2 7 · ³6
```

Challenge 3

Play this game with a partner. Take turns to:

- Choose a number from below and write it down (you can only choose each number once).
- Roll the dice.
- Divide your chosen number by the number on the dice. Choose the most appropriate method to calculate the answer: mental or written.
- Write the calculation and the answer to 2 decimal places. Show any working out.

The person with the smallest answer scores one point. The first person to score five points is the winner.

You will need:
- 0–9 or 1–10 dice

35·6 66·6 62·4 94·5 24·8 49·2 73·5 16·8 53·4 13·4

Unit 8, Week 2, Lesson 2

Dividing decimals using the expanded written method of long division

- Use the expanded written method of long division to divide a decimal by a 2-digit number
- Estimate and check the answer to a calculation

Challenge 1

Find the missing numbers.

a 5·6 × 🍂 = 560
b 3·32 × 🍃 = 332
c 8·7 × 🍁 = 87
d 4·9 × ⭐ = 49
e 6·78 × 🍂 = 678
f 0·47 × ⭐ = 47
g 56·2 × 🍃 = 562
h 0·39 × 🍂 = 39
i 7·59 × 100 = 🍃
j 🍁 × 100 = 345
k 0·03 × 100 = ⭐
l 🍃 × 10 = 21
m 0·19 × 🍂 = 19
n 🍃 × 100 = 46
o 1·11 × 🍃 = 111

Challenge 2

1 For each division calculation write your estimate, then use the expanded written method to work out the answer. Choose your method from the examples given.

Example
58·32 ÷ 18

58·32 ÷ 18 is equivalent to 5832 ÷ 18 ÷ 100

```
        3 2 4
18 | 5 8 3 2
   − 5 4 0 0    (300 × 18)
       4 3 2
   −   3 6 0    (20 × 18)
          7 2
   −      7 2   (4 × 18)
           0
```

324 ÷ 100 = 3·24

```
        3 · 2 4
18 | 5 8 · 3 2
   − 5 4 · 0 0    (300 × 18)
       4 · 3 2
   −   3 · 6 0    (20 × 18)
       0 · 7 2
   −   0 · 7 2    (4 × 18)
       0 · 0 0
```

a 25·2 ÷ 18

b 93·6 ÷ 13

c 68·40 ÷ 15

d 58·86 ÷ 18
e 27·56 ÷ 13
f 68·4 ÷ 19
g 79·42 ÷ 19
h 89·6 ÷ 35
i 15·84 ÷ 33

2 Using each digit only once, make each of the following statements true.

a 0 1 2 3 8   ☐☐·☐ ÷ ☐☐ = 1·6

b 0 1 3 6 8   ☐☐·☐ ÷ ☐☐ = 1·7

c 1 3 4 6 8   ☐☐·☐ ÷ ☐☐ = 2·4

d 1 2 3 4 5   ☐☐·☐ ÷ ☐☐ = 3·8

Hint
Each of the 2-digit numbers is a 'teen' number.

Challenge 3

1 Find the answer to each of these problems.

a 14 friends go to a cafe to celebrate a birthday. The bill comes to a total of €93.52. They share the cost equally between them. How much do they each pay?

b Jasper practises after school for the long jump competition. Each time he practises he jumps 15 times. In one afternoon he jumps a total distance of 78·75 m. What is the average length of each of his jumps?

c Miriam buys 15 m of fabric costing €26.50 per metre and 23 m of another fabric costing €16.25 per metre. Both fabrics are on sale at a 15% discount. How much does she pay in total?

d Marek buys 31 cupcakes to share with his friends. His bill is €74.40 and then he gets 10% off. How much does each cupcake cost him?

2 Write three different situations when you would divide numbers including decimals.

Unit 8, Week 2, Lesson 3

Dividing decimals using the formal written method of long division

- Use the formal written method of long division to divide a decimal by a 2-digit number
- Estimate and check the answer to a calculation

Challenge 1

Copy and complete the table by dividing each number by 10 and 100.

	5	16	32	85	762	20	11	465	3267
÷ 10	0·5								
÷ 100	0·05								

Challenge 2

1 For each division calculation write your estimate, then use the formal written method to work out the answer. Choose your method from the examples shown. Where necessary, round your answers to 2 decimal places.

Example
58·32 ÷ 18

58·32 ÷ 18 is equivalent to 5832 ÷ 18 ÷ 100

```
      3 2 4
18 | 5 8 3 2
    - 5 4 ↓
        4 3
      - 3 6 ↓
          7 2
        - 7 2
            0
```

```
      3 · 2 4
18 | 5 8 · 3 2
    - 5 4 · ↓
        4 · 3
      - 3 · 6 ↓
          0 · 7 2
        - 0 · 7 2
              0
```

324 ÷ 100 = 3·24

a 61·2 ÷ 18
b 41·6 ÷ 13
c 68·79 ÷ 13
d 18·76 ÷ 22
e 91·28 ÷ 14
f 53·43 ÷ 13
g 73·22 ÷ 21
h 52·08 ÷ 14

2 Four shops sell packets of Ginger Snaps. Work out the price that each shop charges for 1 packet of Ginger Snaps.

Bargain Biscuits
15 packets of Ginger Snaps for €54.60

The Ginger Shop
18 packets of Ginger Snaps for €51.66

Cheap Sweets
12 packets of Ginger snaps for €30.24

Everything For Tea
13 packets of Ginger Snaps for €40.04

Challenge 3

1 Timothy sells products round the country. He drives to see each of his clients. Calculate the length of his journey, the speed he travels at, and how long it takes him on average to reach his destination.
Copy and complete the table.
Show your working.

Distance travelled (kilometres)	192·5	583		175	246
Speed travelled (kilometres/h)	55	65	46		
Time taken (h)			19	25	6

2 Write three of your own word problems using the information in the table above. Give them to a friend to solve. Check if their answers to the word problems match your answers in the table.

Unit 8, Week 2, Lesson 4

Solving word problems (3)

- Solve word problems rounding answers to a suitable degree of accuracy where necessary
- Estimate and check the answer to a calculation

Challenge 1

Follow the instructions to find the final number.

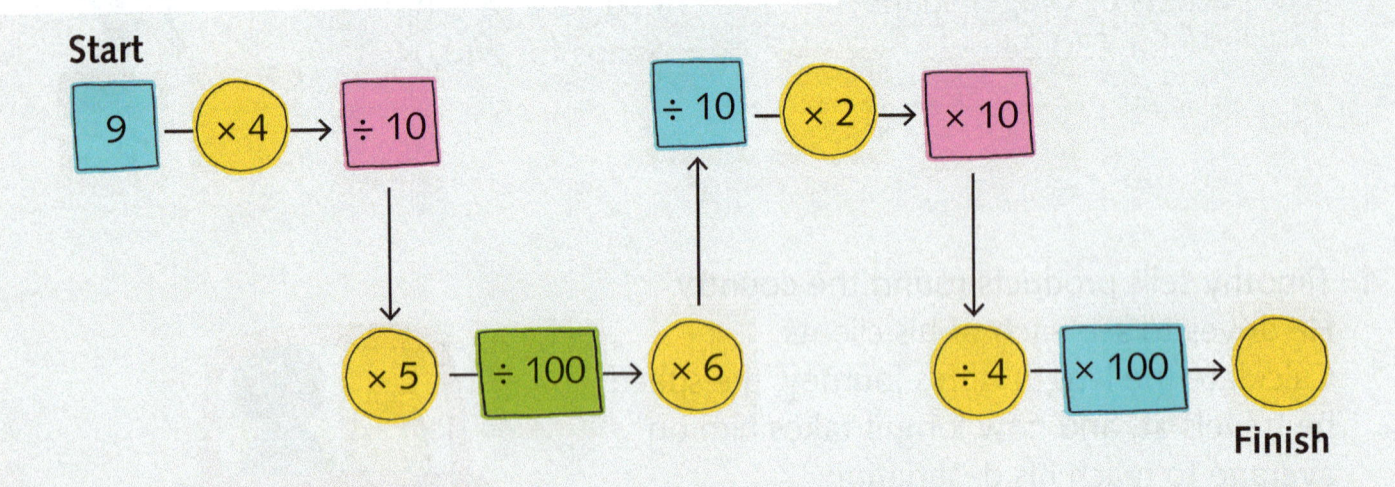

Start

9 → ×4 → ÷10 → ×5 → ÷100 → ×6 → ÷10 → ×2 → ×10 → ÷4 → ×100 → **Finish**

Challenge 2

Find the answer to each of these questions about a sewing and fabric shop, rounding your answer appropriately if necessary. Remember to use estimation to check your answers.

a Jagdish buys 65·1 m of fabric. He cuts it into 3 even pieces. What is the length of each piece? If a suit can be made from 4 m of fabric, how many suits can be made from each piece?

b If elastic costs €3.56 per metre, how much does it cost for 60 cm of elastic?

c The sewing and fabric shop sells different coloured ribbons in metre lengths. Laura pays €64.32 for 12 metres of purple ribbon. How much does the ribbon cost per metre?

d Zips cost €9.65 per tub. Ben buys 6 tubs. He takes a €50 note out of his wallet. How much more money does he need?

e There are 33·58 m of curtain material remaining. If each set of curtains requires 5 m of fabric, how many sets of curtains can be made?

f Kara buys a sewing machine for €87.40. She receives a 25% discount in the sale. How much does she pay for her sewing machine?

g Which costs more per button: a tub of 24 buttons at 26c each or a tub of 18 buttons for €6.48?

h Conran buys 22 boxes of sequins. He pays €18.70 in total. How much does 1 box of sequins cost?

2 Look carefully at the answers to each of the questions in Question 1. Work out how much money the sewing and fabric shop has taken in total from all the customers who have made a purchase.

Challenge 3

1 Write an explanation for each of the following.

a How can you use money to show how to divide 1 by 4?

b Why does finding the cost of items usually include multiplying and dividing of whole numbers and decimals?

c Explain how 5·2 × 1·7 is similar to the calculation 52 × 17.

d Explain how multiplying and dividing decimals is similar to calculating with whole numbers.

2 Make up a word problem to match the calculation 10·98 ÷ 3.

Unit 8, Week 3, Lesson 1

Perimeter and area

Know that shapes with the same perimeters can have different areas and vice versa

Challenge 1

Each small square is 1 cm across. For each shape find:
- the perimeter in centimetres (cm)
- the area in square centimetres (cm^2)

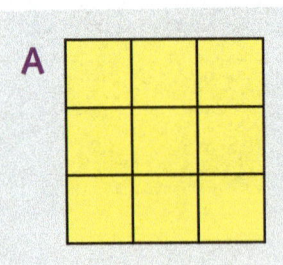

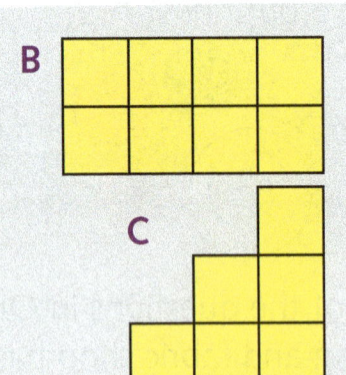

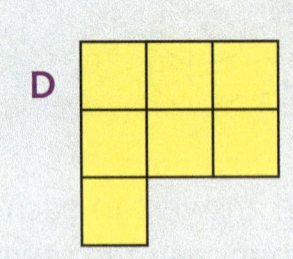

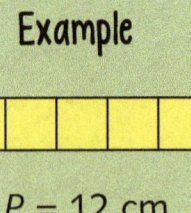

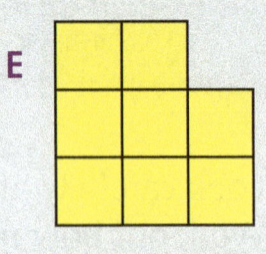

Example

$P = 12$ cm
$A = 5$ cm^2

A   B   C   D   E

Challenge 2

1. Each small square is 1 cm across. Find the area and perimeter of each of the blue shaded shapes.

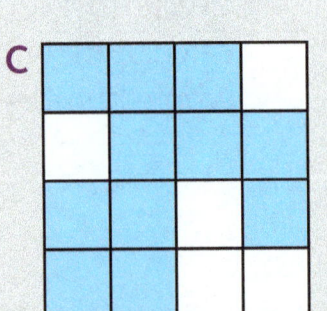

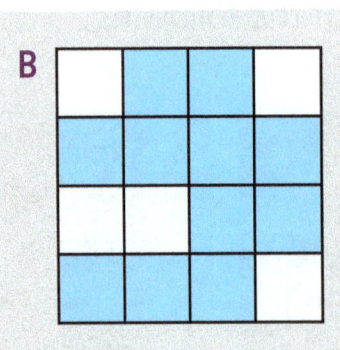

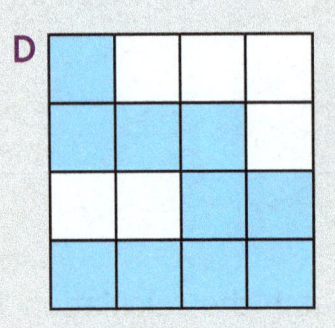

Example

$A = 12$ cm^2
$P = 20$ cm

A   B   C   D

2 Using Resource 57: Equal perimeters, draw six shapes that have a perimeter of 20 cm and find the area of each one.

You will need:
- Resource 57: Equal perimeters
- ruler

3 Peter bought 24 square slabs measuring 1 metre by 1 metre to tile his patio. Find the perimeter and area of his patio for each rectangle of 24 slabs.

   a 12 m long by 2 m wide   b 8 m long by 3 m wide   c 6 m long by 4 m wide

4 A landscape gardener ordered 60 square slabs measuring 1 metre by 1 metre. List the different rectangular arrangements he can make. Then write the perimeter and area of each rectangle.

Challenge 3

1 A farmer has 40 metres of fencing to make a rectangular enclosure in his barn for his sheep and lambs.

Example
16 m × 4 m
$P = 40$ m
$A = 64$ m^2

   a List all the possible measurements for his rectangular enclosure in whole metres.

   b Which measurements will give the largest area for the sheep and lambs?

2 The farmer considers using one wall of the barn for one side of the enclosure and 40 metres of fencing for the other three sides. What is the largest rectangular area he can enclose with his fencing?

Key
barn wall
fencing

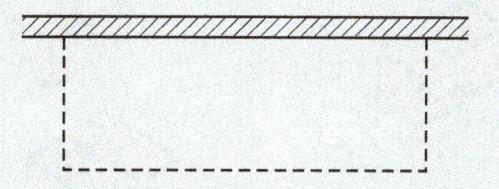

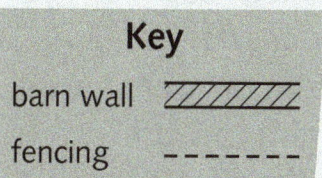

3 His son suggests that he could use two walls of the barn that are at right angles for two sides of the enclosure and use the 40 metres of fencing for the other two sides. What is the largest rectangular area he can enclose with his fencing?

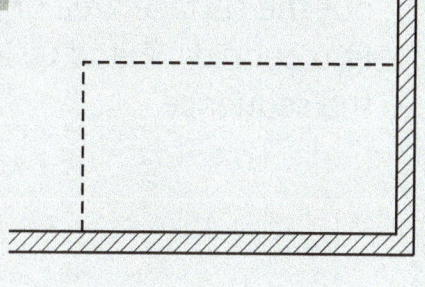

Unit 8, Week 3, Lesson 2

Surface area

Know when to use the formula for the area of shapes

Challenge 1

Find the surface area of each cuboid by counting the squares.

A

B

Example

Visible 1 cm squares: 8

Hidden 1 cm squares: 8

Surface area = 16 cm^2

Challenge 2

1. Each net of a 3-D shape is drawn on 1 cm squared paper. Calculate the surface area of each net in square centimetres.

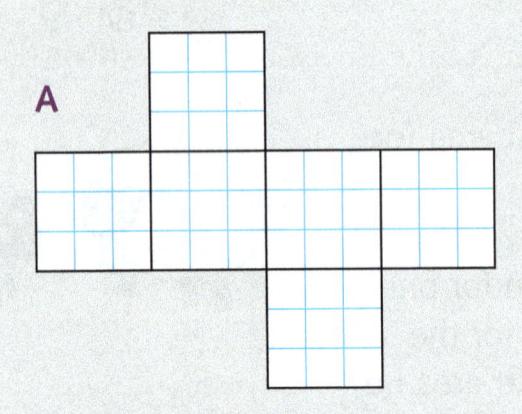

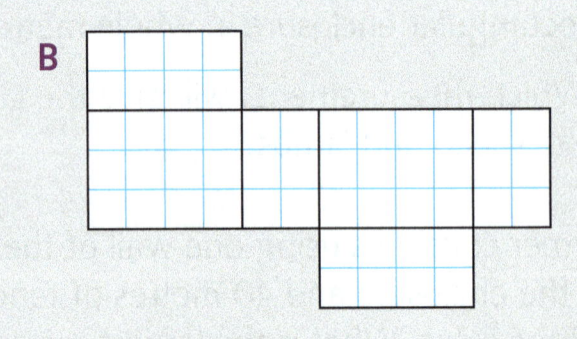

A

B

2. Calculate the surface area of each cuboid and record your answers in a table. Look for a pattern in your results and use the pattern to work out the surface area of the next two cuboids, F and G, in the sequence.

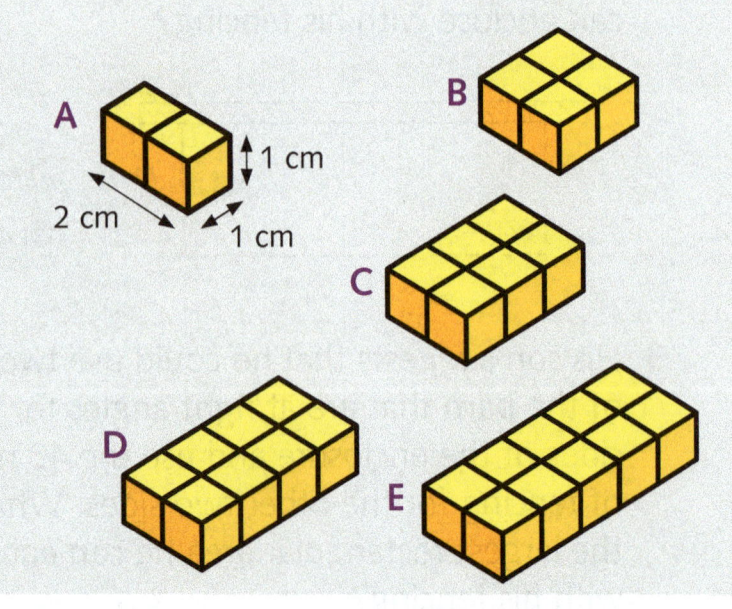

A — 2 cm, 1 cm, 1 cm

B

C

D

E

94

3 Each cube is built using 1 cm³ cubes. Copy and complete the table below.

You will need:
- ruler

Length of one side (cm)	1	2	3	4
Surface area of one face (cm²)	1			
Surface area of the cube (cm²)	6			

4 Using your table from Question 3, find the surface area of cubes with sides of:

a 5 cm   b 8 cm   c 10 cm

5 Calculate the surface area of each box below. The boxes are not drawn to scale.

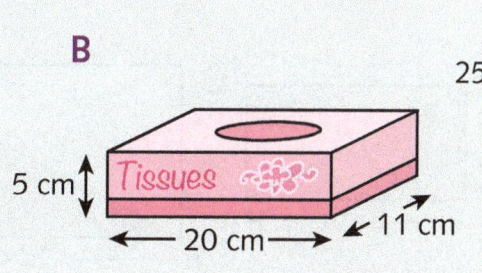

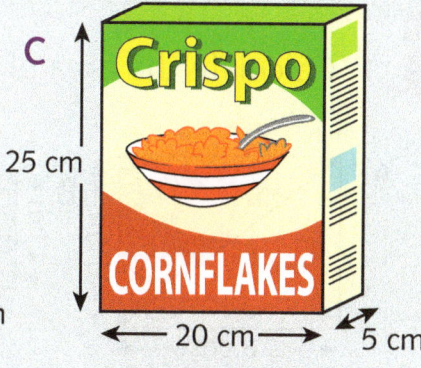

A: 10 cm, 20 cm, 10 cm (TEA BAGS)
B: 5 cm, 20 cm, 11 cm (Tissues)
C: 25 cm, 20 cm, 5 cm (Crispo CORNFLAKES)

Challenge 3

These cubes are made using alternate red and yellow 1 cm³ cubes. For each cube, work out the total surface area that is red and the total surface area that is yellow.

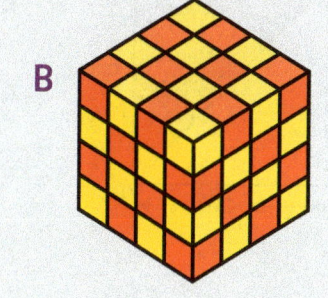

A   B

Unit 8, Week 3, Lesson 3

Area of triangles

Calculate the area of a triangle using the rule $A = \frac{1}{2}bh$

Challenge 1

1. Find the area of each blue triangle. Each small square is 1 cm across.

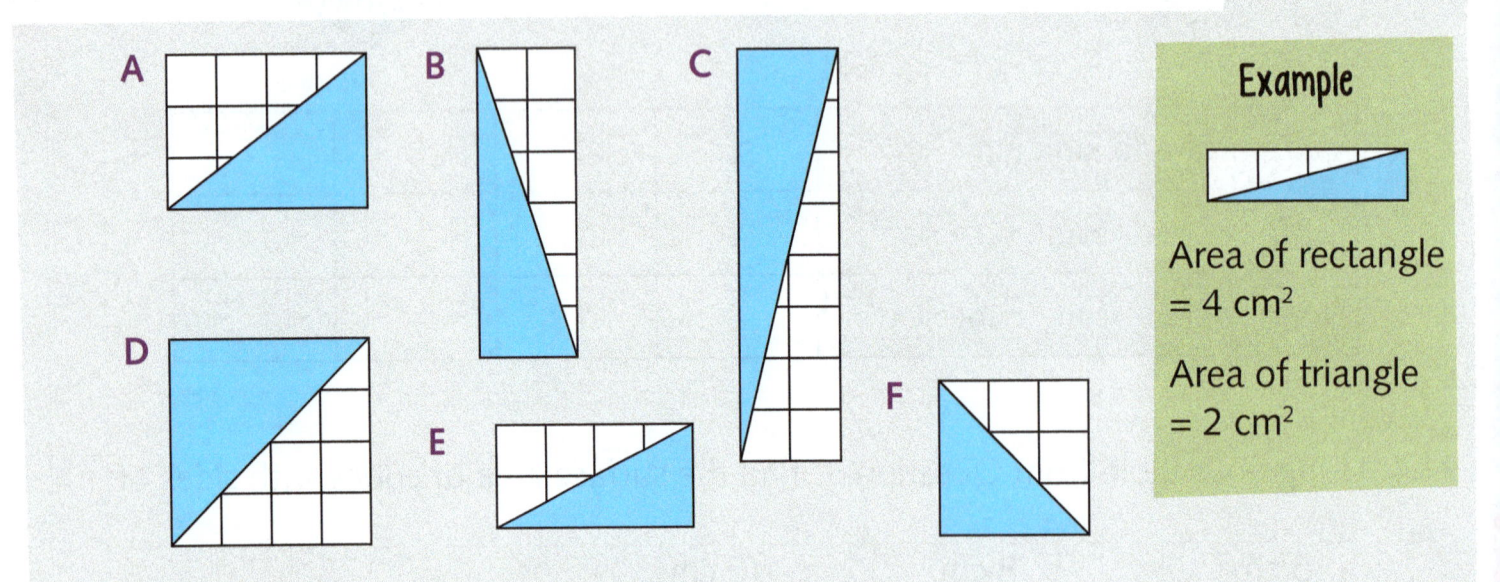

Example

Area of rectangle = 4 cm²

Area of triangle = 2 cm²

2. Write the letter of the triangle that has the same area as triangle D.

Challenge 2

1. Calculate the area of each purple triangle using the rule $A = \frac{1}{2}bh$.

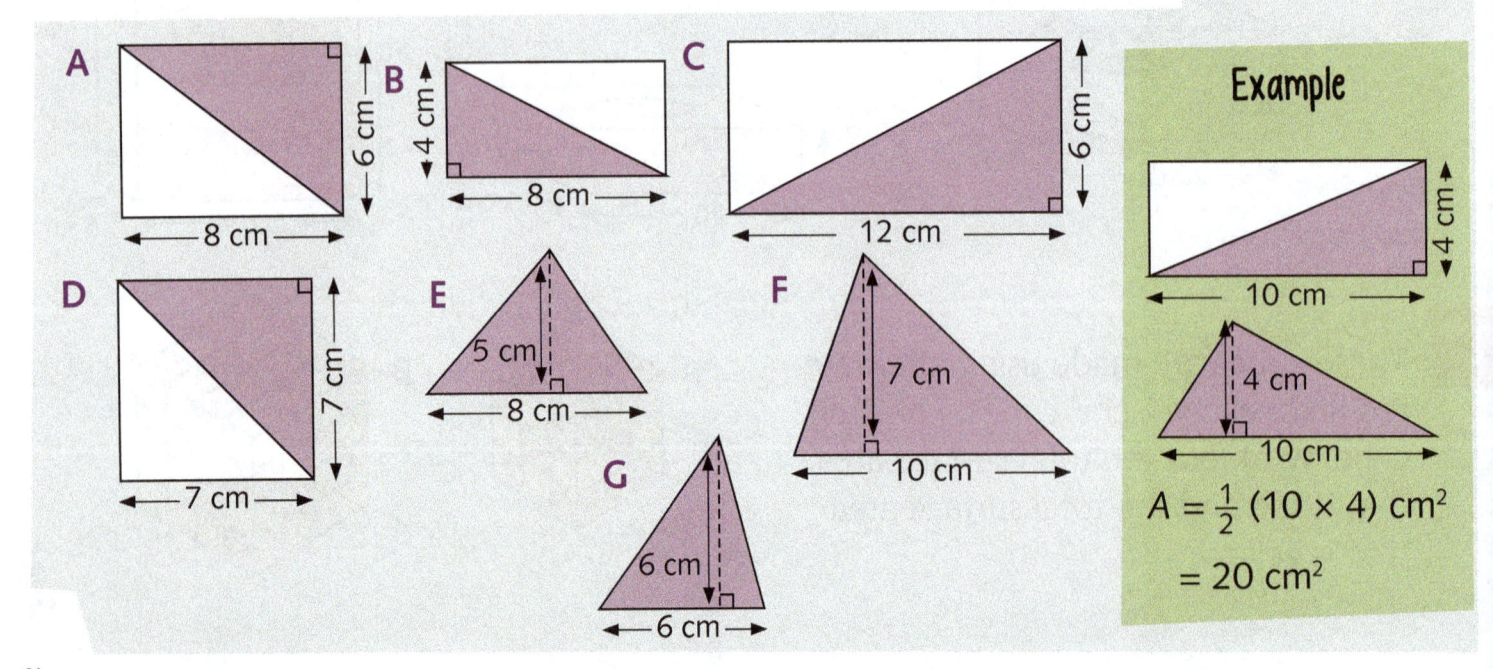

Example

10 cm, 4 cm

$A = \frac{1}{2}(10 \times 4)$ cm²

= 20 cm²

A: 8 cm, 6 cm
B: 8 cm, 4 cm
C: 12 cm, 6 cm
D: 7 cm, 7 cm
E: 8 cm, 5 cm
F: 10 cm, 7 cm
G: 6 cm, 6 cm

96

2 Turn triangles into rectangles.

- Copy each yellow triangle onto 1 cm squared paper and cut it out.
- Make one cut at the midpoint of the longest side. Transform your triangle into a rectangle.
- Glue each rectangle in your exercise book or on a piece of paper.
- Write the area of each rectangle.

You will need:
- 1 cm squared paper
- ruler
- scissors
- glue

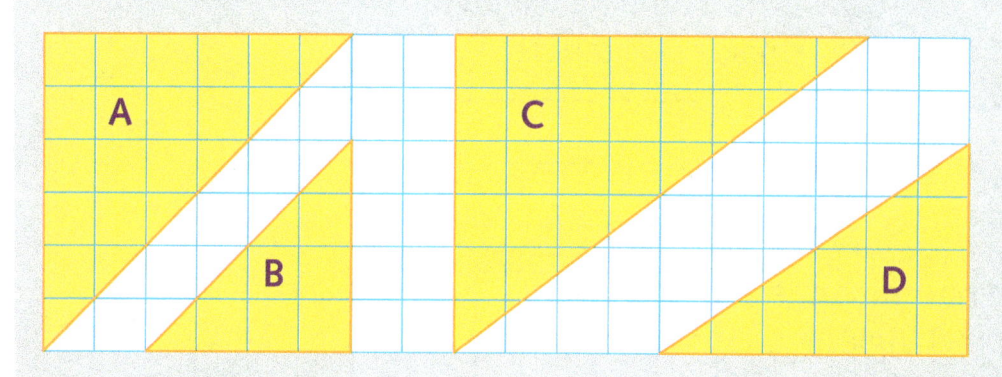

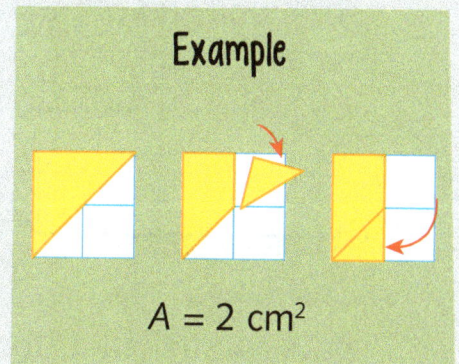

Example

$A = 2$ cm^2

Challenge 3

You can find the area of the red triangle by subtracting the area of the pieces outside the triangle from the area of the square. Calculate the area of these red triangles in cm^2. Show the steps in your working. The dots are 1 cm apart.

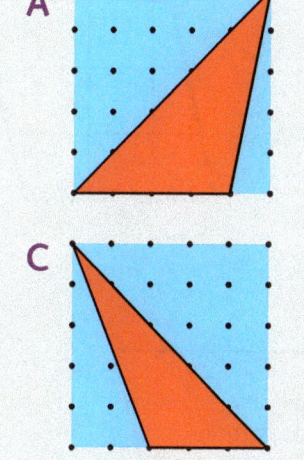

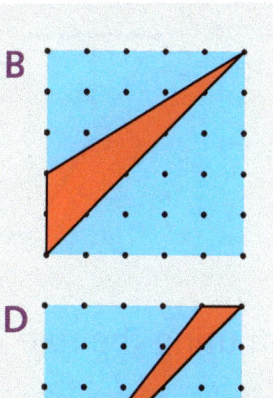

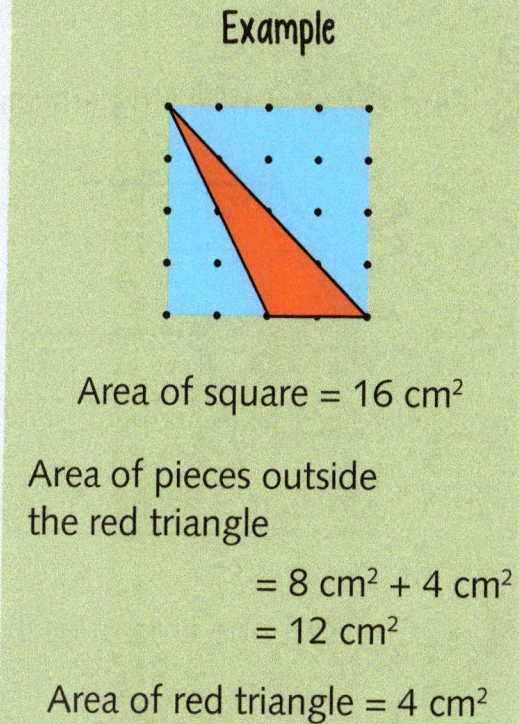

Example

Area of square = 16 cm^2

Area of pieces outside the red triangle
$$= 8 \text{ cm}^2 + 4 \text{ cm}^2$$
$$= 12 \text{ cm}^2$$

Area of red triangle = 4 cm^2

Unit 8, Week 3, Lesson 4

Area of parallelograms

Calculate the area of a parallelogram using the rule $A = bh$ and relate the dissection of a rectangle to the area of a parallelogram

Rule

Finding the area of parallelograms:

- Cut a right-angled triangle from one end of the parallelogram.
- Slide the triangle to the other side of the parallelogram to make a rectangle.

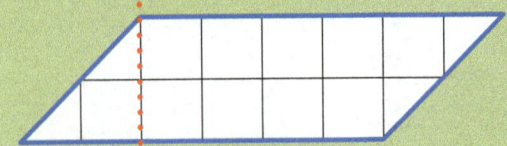

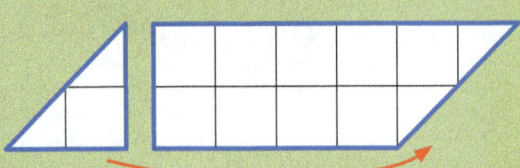

- The parallelogram now has the same base and height as the rectangle. So you can use the rule $A = bh$.

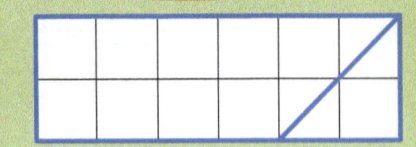

$A = bh$
$= (6 \times 2)$ cm^2
$= 12$ cm^2

Challenge 1

Find the area of each parallelogram in cm^2. Each grid square is 1 cm across.

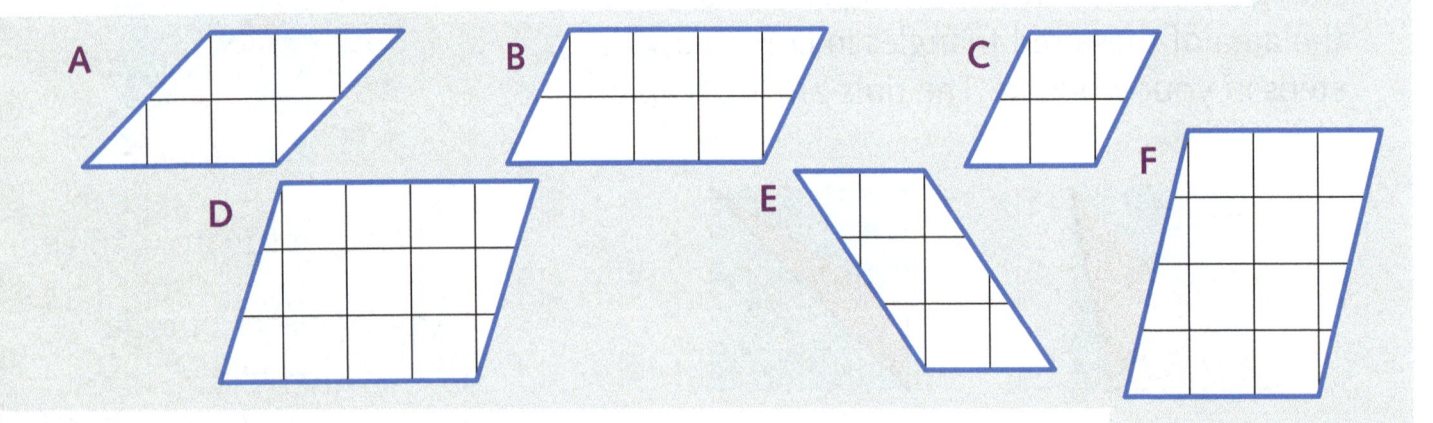

A   B   C   D   E   F

Challenge 2

1 Calculate the area of each parallelogram using the rule $A = bh$.

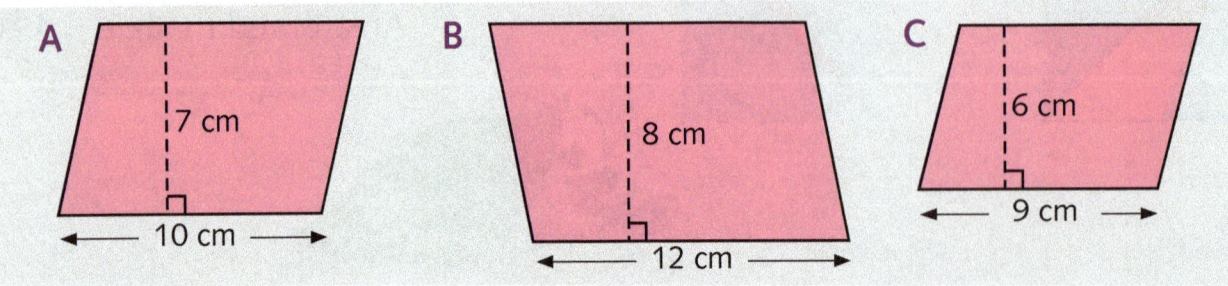

A: 7 cm, 10 cm
B: 8 cm, 12 cm
C: 6 cm, 9 cm

98

2 Copy shapes A to D onto 1 cm square dot paper.

a Draw and letter the next two parallelograms in the sequence.

b Copy and complete the table for the area of each shape.

Shape	A	B	C	D	E	F
Area (cm²)						

3 Copy the shapes P, Q and R onto 1 cm square dot paper.

a Draw and letter the next three parallelograms in the sequence.

b Copy and complete the table below for the area of each shape.

c Explain the pattern.

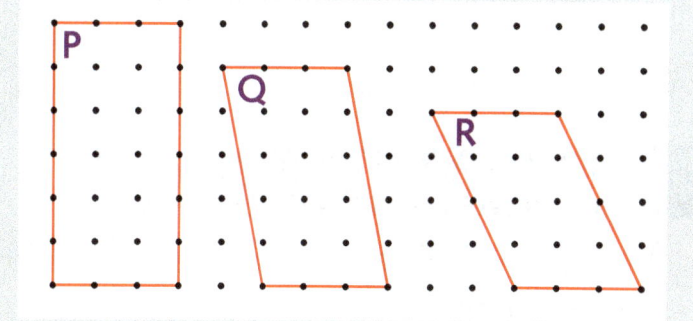

Shape	P	Q	R	S	T	U
Area (cm²)						

You will need:
- 1 cm squared dot paper
- ruler

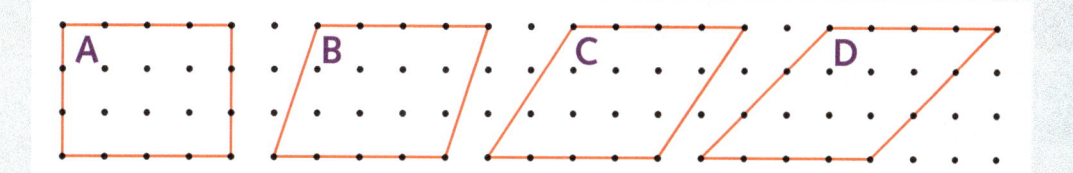

Challenge 3

Use what you know about finding the area of a parallelogram to find the area of each isosceles trapezium.

A: 9 cm (top), 6 cm (height), 3 cm and 3 cm (bottom extensions)

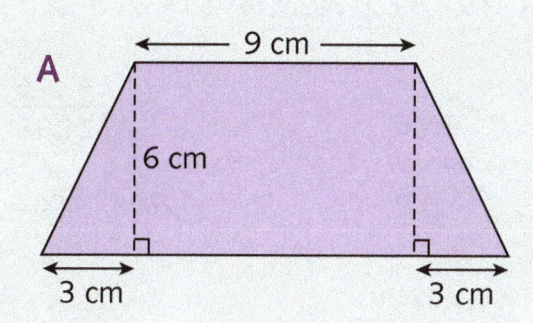

B: 15 cm (top), 7 cm (height), 10 cm (bottom)

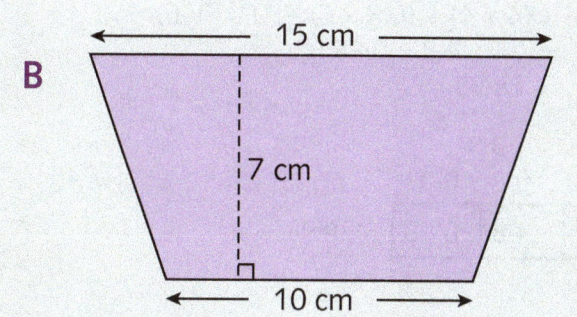

Maths facts

Addition and subtraction

Whole numbers

Example: 456 287 + 359 849

```
   456 287
 + 359 849
   -------
   816 136
   1 1 1  11
```

Example: 746 291 − 298 354

```
   ⁶7⁴⁶6 ²9¹1  (746 291 with borrows: 6 13 15 12 8 11)
 − 298 354
   -------
   447 937
```

Decimals

Example: 57·486 + 45·378

```
   57·486
 + 45·378
  -------
  102·864
   1  11
```

Example: 63·237 − 45·869

```
   63·237   (with borrows: 5 12 11 12 17)
 − 45·869
   ------
   17·368
```

Multiplication and division

Written methods – short multiplication

Whole numbers

Example: 5643 × 8

Formal written method
```
    5643
  ×    8
   ⁵³²
  -----
   45144
```

Decimals

Example: 4·83 × 6

Partitioning

4·83 × 6 = (4 × 6) + (0·8 × 6) + (0·03 × 6)
         = 24 + 4·8 + 0·18
         = 28·98

Grid method

×	4	0·8	0·03
6	24	4·8	0·18

= 28·98

Expanded written method

4·83 × 6 is equivalent to 483 × 6 ÷ 100

```
    483
  ×   6
  -----
     18  ( 3 × 6)
    480  ( 80 × 6)
   2400  (400 × 6)
  -----
   2898
```

2898 ÷ 100 = 28·98

Formal written method

```
    483
  ×  ⁴¹6
  -----
   2898
```

2898 ÷ 100 = 28·98

100

Written methods – long multiplication
Whole numbers

Example: 285 × 63

Partitioning

285 × 63 = (200 × 63) + (80 × 63) + (5 × 63)
= 12 600 + 5040 + 315
= 17 955

Grid method

×	200	80	5
60	12 000	4800	300
3	600	240	15

   17 100
+   855
   17 955

Expanded written method

```
    285              or        285
  ×  63                      ×  63
  17⁵¹300 (285 × 60)          8²⁵¹5 (285 × 3)
    8²5¹5 (285 × 3)          17⁵¹300 (285 × 60)
  17955                      17955
```

Formal written method

```
    285
  ×  63
    8²5¹5
  17⁵¹300
  17955
```

Decimals

Example: 7·56 × 34

Partitioning

7·56 × 34 = (7 × 34) + (0·5 × 34) + (0·06 × 34)
= 238 + 17 + 2·04
= 257·04

Grid method

×	7	0·5	0·06
30	210	15	1·8
4	28	2	0·24

  226·80
+ 30·24
  257·04
    1

Expanded written method

7·56 × 34 is equivalent to 756 × 34 ÷ 100

```
    756              or       756
  ×  34                     ×  34
  22¹6¹80 (756 × 30)         30²²4 (756 × 4)
    30²²4 (756 × 4)        22¹6¹80 (756 × 30)
  25704                    25704
    1                        1
```

25 704 ÷ 100 = 257·04   25 704 ÷ 100 = 257·04

Formal written method

7·56 × 34 is equivalent to 756 × 34 ÷ 100

```
    756
  ×  34
   30²²4
  22¹6¹80
  25704
    1
```

25 704 ÷ 100 = 257·04

Written methods – short division
Whole numbers

Example: 1838 ÷ 8

Whole number remainder

```
     2 2 9 r 6
8 ) 1 8 ²3 ⁷8
```

Fraction remainder

```
     2 2 9 ¾
8 ) 1 8 ²3 ⁷8
```

Decimal remainder

```
     2 2 9 · 7 5
8 ) 1 8 ²3 ⁷8 · ⁶0 ⁴0
```

Decimals

> Example: 45·36 ÷ 6

45·36 ÷ 6 is equivalent to 4536 ÷ 6 ÷ 100

```
      7 · 5 6                  7  5 6
  6)4 5 ·³3 ³6     or      6)4 5³3 ³6
                             756 ÷ 100 = 7·56
```

Written methods – long division

Whole numbers

> Example: 5836 ÷ 18

Expanded written method

```
         3 2 4 r 4
   18)5 8 3 6
     - 5 4 0 0    (300 × 18)
       ³4 ¹³3 6
     -   3 6 0    ( 20 × 18)
           7 6
     -     7 2    (  4 × 18)
             4
```

5836 ÷ 18 = 324 r 4 or $324\frac{2}{9}$

Formal written method

```
         3 2 4 r 4
   18)5 8 3 6
     - 5 4↓
         4 3
       - 3 6↓
           7 6
         - 7 2
             4
```

5836 ÷ 18 = 324 r 4 or $324\frac{2}{9}$

Decimals

> Example: 58·32 ÷ 18

Expanded written method

58·32 ÷ 18 is equivalent to 5832 ÷ 18 ÷ 100

```
         3 2 4                                    3 · 2 4
   18)5 8 3 2                                18)5 8 · 3 2
     - 5 4 0 0   (300 × 18)    or             - 5 4 · 0 0   (  3  × 18)
       ³4 ¹³3 2                                  ³4 · ¹³3 2
     -   3 6 0   ( 20 × 18)                   -   3 · 6 0   (0·2  × 18)
           7 2                                      0 · 7 2
     -     7 2   (  4 × 18)                   -     0 · 7 2 (0·04 × 18)
             0                                        0 · 0 0
```

324 ÷ 100 = 3·24

Formal written method

58·32 ÷ 18 is equivalent to 5832 ÷ 18 ÷ 100

$$
\begin{array}{r}
324 \\
18 \overline{\smash{)}5832} \\
-54\downarrow \\
\hline
43 \\
-36\downarrow \\
\hline
72 \\
-72 \\
\hline
0
\end{array}
\qquad \text{or} \qquad
\begin{array}{r}
3·24 \\
18 \overline{\smash{)}58·32} \\
-54\downarrow \\
\hline
4·3 \\
-3·6\downarrow \\
\hline
0·72 \\
-0·72 \\
\hline
0
\end{array}
$$

324 ÷ 100 = 3·24

Fractions, decimals and percentages

$\dfrac{1}{100} = 0·01 = 1\%$ $\dfrac{2}{100} = \dfrac{1}{50} = 0·02 = 2\%$ $\dfrac{4}{100} = \dfrac{1}{25} = 0·04 = 4\%$

$\dfrac{5}{100} = \dfrac{1}{20} = 0·05 = 5\%$ $\dfrac{10}{100} = \dfrac{1}{10} = 0·1 = 10\%$ $\dfrac{20}{100} = \dfrac{1}{5} = 0·2 = 20\%$

$\dfrac{25}{100} = \dfrac{1}{4} = 0·25 = 25\%$ $\dfrac{40}{100} = \dfrac{2}{5} = 0·4 = 40\%$ $\dfrac{50}{100} = \dfrac{1}{2} = 0·5 = 50\%$

$\dfrac{75}{100} = \dfrac{3}{4} = 0·75 = 75\%$ $\dfrac{80}{100} = \dfrac{4}{5} = 0·8 = 80\%$ $\dfrac{100}{100} = \dfrac{10}{10} = 1 = 100\%$

$\dfrac{2}{5} + \dfrac{4}{5} = \dfrac{6}{5}$ $\dfrac{7}{8} - \dfrac{3}{8} = \dfrac{4}{8}$ $\dfrac{2}{3} \times 4 = \dfrac{2}{3} \times \dfrac{4}{1}$ $2\dfrac{3}{4} \times 3 = \dfrac{11}{4} \times 3$

$= 1\dfrac{1}{5}$ $= \dfrac{1}{2}$ $= \dfrac{2 \times 4}{3 \times 1}$ $= \dfrac{11 \times 3}{4 \times 1}$

$= \dfrac{8}{3}$ $= \dfrac{33}{4}$

$= 2\dfrac{2}{3}$ $= 8\dfrac{1}{4}$

$9\dfrac{2}{3} + 6\dfrac{4}{5}$ $11\dfrac{3}{4} - 7\dfrac{2}{6}$ $\dfrac{1}{2} \times \dfrac{3}{4} = \dfrac{1 \times 3}{2 \times 4}$ $\dfrac{2}{3} \div 4 = \dfrac{2}{3 \times 4}$

$9 + 6 = 15$ $11 - 7 = 4$ $= \dfrac{3}{8}$ $= \dfrac{2}{12}$

$\dfrac{2}{3} + \dfrac{4}{5} = \dfrac{10}{15} + \dfrac{12}{15}$ $\dfrac{3}{4} - \dfrac{2}{6} = \dfrac{9}{12} - \dfrac{4}{12}$ $= \dfrac{1}{6}$

$= \dfrac{22}{15}$ $= \dfrac{5}{12}$

$= 1\dfrac{7}{15}$ $\dfrac{5}{12} + 4 = 4\dfrac{5}{12}$

$1\dfrac{7}{15} + 15 = 16\dfrac{7}{15}$

103

Measurement

Length

1 km = 1000 m = 100 000 cm
0·1 km = 100 m = 10 000 cm = 100 000 mm
0·01 km = 10 m = 1000 cm = 10 000 mm
1 m = 100 cm = 1000 mm
0·1 m = 10 cm = 100 mm

0·01 m = 1 cm = 10 mm
0·001 m = 0·1 cm = 1 mm
1 cm = 10 mm
0·1 cm = 1 mm

Metric units and imperial units – Length

1 km ≈ $\frac{5}{8}$ miles (8 km ≈ 5 miles)
1 inch ≈ 2·5 cm

Capacity

1 litre = 1000 ml
0·1 l = 100 ml
0·01 l = 10 ml
0·001 l = 1 ml
1 cl = 10 ml

24-hour time

Perimeter, area and volume

P = perimeter   A = area   V = volume
l = length   w = width   b = base   h = height

Perimeter of a rectangle
P = 2(l + w)

Perimeter of a square
P = 4 × l or   P = 4l

Area of a rectangle
A = l × w   or   A = lw

Area of a triangle
A = $\frac{1}{2}$ × b × h   or   A = $\frac{1}{2}$bh

Area of a parallelogram
A = b × h   or   A = bh

Volume of a cuboid
V = l × w × h   or   V = $l$wh

Mass

1 t = 1000 kg   1 kg = 1000 g   0·1 kg = 100 g   0·01 kg = 10 g   0·001 kg = 1 g

Geometry

Parts of a circle

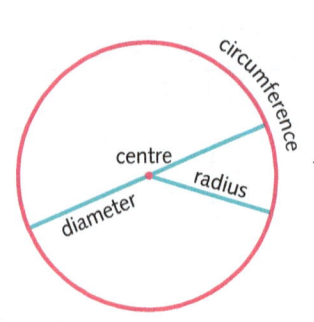

circumference, centre, radius, diameter

Coordinates

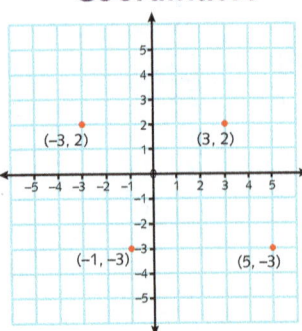

(−3, 2)   (3, 2)
(−1, −3)   (5, −3)

Translation

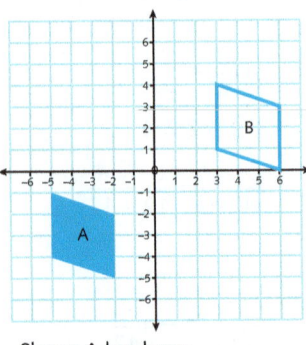

Shape A has been translated 8 squares to the right and 5 squares up.

Reflection

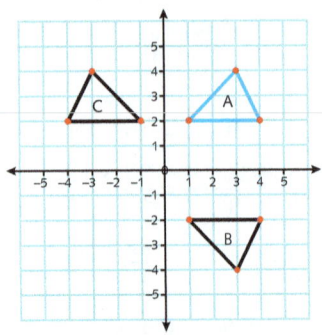

Shape A has been reflected in the x-axis (Shape B) and in the y-axis (Shape C).